Best Bush and Beach Walks of the Gold Coast

By
Alan Ernst

Woodslane Press Pty Ltd
10 Apollo Street
Warriewood, NSW 2102
Email: info@woodslane.com.au
Tel: 02 8445 2300 Website: www.walks.com.au

First published in Australia in 2015 by Woodslane Press
© 2015 Woodslane Press, text © 2015 Alan Ernst

This work is copyright. All rights reserved. Apart from any fair dealing for the purposes of study, research or review, as permitted under Australian copyright law, no part of this publication may be reproduced, distributed, or transmitted in any other form or by any means, including photocopying, recording, or other electronic or mechanical methods, without the prior written permission of the publisher. For permission requests, write to the publisher, addressed "Attention: Permissions Coordinator", at the address above.

The information in this publication is based upon the current state of commercial and industry practice and the general circumstances as at the date of publication. Every effort has been made to obtain permissions relating to information reproduced in this publication. The publisher makes no representations as to the accuracy, reliability or completeness of the information contained in this publication. To the extent permitted by law, the publisher excludes all conditions, warranties and other obligations in relation to the supply of this publication and otherwise limits its liability to the recommended retail price. In no circumstances will the publisher be liable to any third party for any consequential loss or damage suffered by any person resulting in any way from the use or reliance on this publication or any part of it. Any opinions and advice contained in the publication are offered solely in pursuance of the author's and publisher's intention to provide information, and have not been specifically sought.

National Library of Australia Cataloguing-in-Publication entry

Creator:	Ernst, Alan, author.
Title:	Best Bush and Beach Walks of the Gold Coast: the full colour guide to 33 fantastic walks / Alan Ernst.
ISBN:	9781921683299 (paperback)
Notes:	Includes index.
Subjects:	Trails--Queensland--Gold Coast Region--Guidebooks.
	Trails--Queensland--Gold Coast Region--Pictorial works.
	Nature trails--Queensland--Gold Coast Region--Guidebooks.
	Nature trails--Queensland--Gold Coast Region--Pictorial works.
	Beaches--Queensland--Gold Coast Region--Guidebooks
	Beaches--Queensland--Gold Coast Region--Pictorial works.
Dewey Number:	796.51099432

Printed in Australia by the OPUS Group
Designed by Ryan Morrison Design

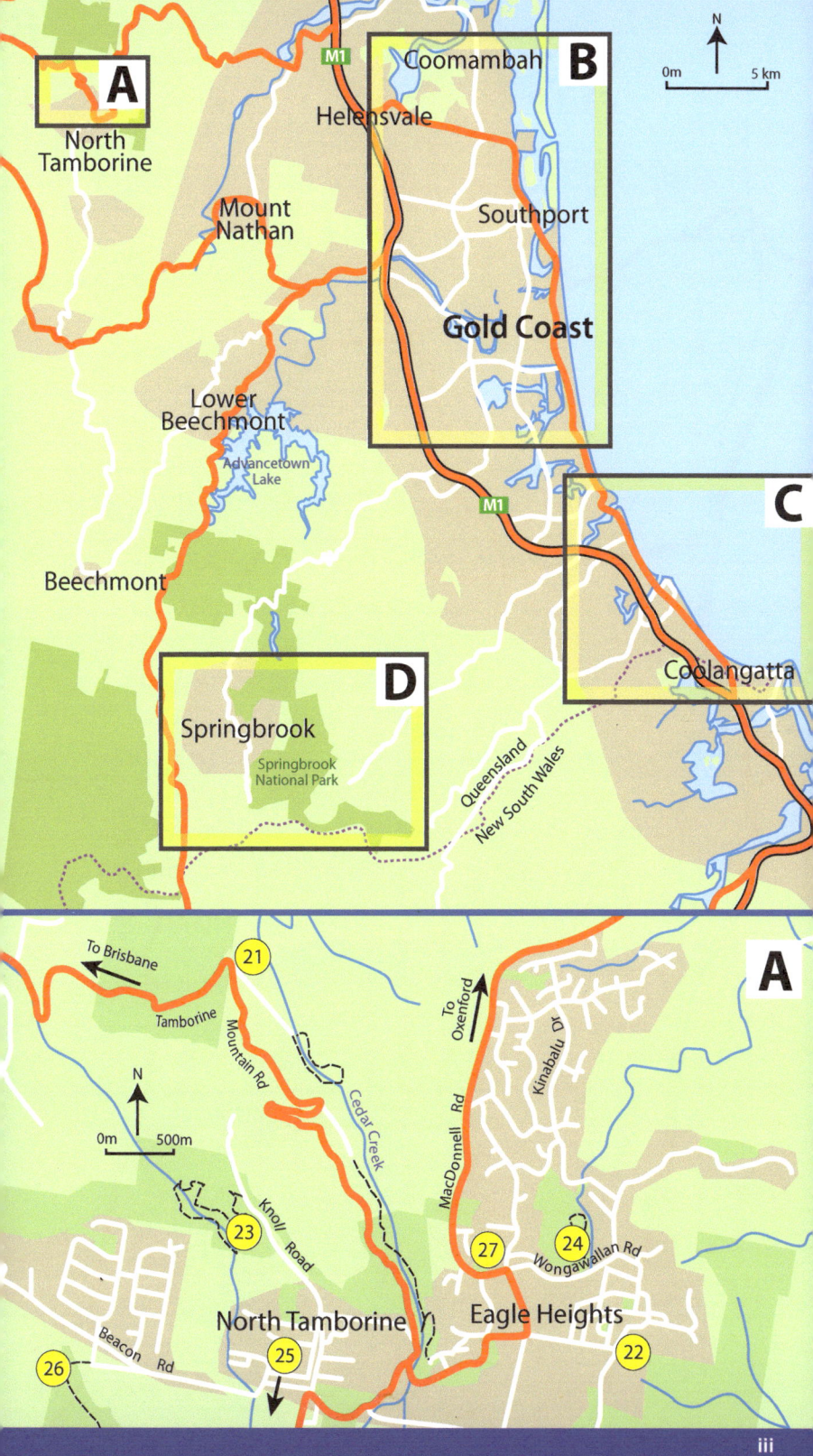

iii

Contents

Location Maps .... iii-v
Introduction 2
    Public transport 2
    Walk grades and times 3
    Walking with children 3
    Taking your dog 4
    Track closures 4
    Looking after the environment 5
    Safety 5
    Gold Coast Oceanway 7
Walks at a Glance 8-11
Best Bush and Beach Walks of the Gold Coast
    Coastal Walks North 12
    Beyond the Beach: North 40
    Southern Gold Coast 66
    Hinterland North: Tambourine 100
    Hinterland South: Springbrook 130
Gold Coast Wildlife 157
Index 158
Photography in this book 160
About the Author & Acknowledgements 161
Map Symbols 162
Other Books from Woodslane 164
Feedback Page 170

Introduction

Welcome to the Gold Coast, famous for its long golden beaches, endless sunshine, and seemingly even more endless night-life. What you may not know is that it's also a place where you can enjoy a diverse range of walks, from leisurely strolls along the beachfront to rugged hikes in the mountainous hinterland. With a coastline stretching from Point Danger on the Queensland/New South Wales border to the Gold Coast Seaway, many of the walks offer fabulous ocean views, the chance to explore the rocky headlands, and the opportunity to experience some of the world's greatest surf beaches. Tucked in beside the towering architecture of the coast's tourist hotels, you'll still find a few remaining fibro beach shacks – a legacy of a bygone era. There are also other reminders of the Gold Coast's history, in the form of historic buildings, markers of maritime dramas and tributes to those who contributed to the community and culture of the area.

Away from the beaches, the parks and gardens provide welcome shade and a retreat from the sun and the sand. Just a short drive inland takes you to the Gold Coast Hinterland, with its lush rainforest parks, charming mountain villages and a landscape barely touched by humans. Walks here meander through ancient rainforests, with magnificent mountain vistas, tumbling waterfalls, and spectacular wildlife. It's a nature lover's paradise, with the chance to see kangaroos, possums, koalas, bowerbirds and rainbow-coloured parrots. In between walks it's also possible to relax and revive in one of the many cafés which line the streets of the area's pretty mountain villages.

Public transport

Many of the walks in this book can be accessed by public transport, although for some, particularly in the hinterland areas, you will need a car. The Gold Coast is serviced by Surfside Buslines and in part by Gold Coast Light Rail. In some cases, exact bus routes aren't listed in the *At a Glance* section of each walk because there are simply too many options and route numbers will depend on where you are travelling from.

Introduction

You can get a copy of *Surfside's Get Around* Guide on their buses, at information centres or on their website, at www.surfside.com.au. Detailed timetables are available via the Translink website at www.translink.com.au or by phoning 13 12 30.

Walk grades and times

Every walk includes the grade and time needed. These are estimates and the time taken will depend on the speed you walk, and how long you stop to view the scenery. With children, it may take longer as they will wish to stop at playgrounds and other points of interest. You will soon work out if your pace is faster or slower than the times indicated and adjust your outing to suit.

Walk grades are based on the Australian National Track Grading System which has standardised levels of difficulty ranging from Grades 1 to 5, where 1 is the easiest. Grade 1 tracks can be accessed by wheelchair and grade 5 tracks are for very experienced bushwalkers only. The walks in this guide range from grade 1-2, described as **Easy**, to grades 3 or **Medium** and 4 or **Hard**.

Grading is based on the most difficult sections of the walk. In some case you can skip the more difficult sections.

Easy – Fairly smooth with little ascent or descent, suitable for all ages but take care with children.

Medium – May contain steep sections with loose or rough ground or lots of steps.

Hard – For experienced walkers with a high level of fitness and competent navigation skills. Have a minimum of two, and preferably three, people in the group and be sure to let others know of your route and expected time of return.

Walking with children

Many of the walks in this book are suitable for children, however, only a parent will know if distances and grades are suitable for their child. Often a combination of walking, riding in a backpack, being pushed in a stroller or riding a tricycle is good for young children.

Many of the walks have unfenced or limited fencing on sections near water or steep drops, and close supervision is required. The same applies where walks are near roads and car parks.

Many of the concrete footpaths, particularly along the foreshore, are

Introduction

shared with cyclists. Keep a careful lookout for bike riders, and keep children on your left. Check for signage which indicates where particular parts of the path are designated to separate cyclists and walkers.

Many young children, with some encouragement, will show interest in fallen leaves, sticks, small rocks, shells and other 'treasures' along the way (but remember that it is illegal to remove shells or plants from national parks). Some of the walks also pass close by playgrounds, beaches or other attractions.

Take snacks and drinks for children and have regular rests. Older children often enjoy family walks if they take a friend along. Being given the job of taking photos during the walk can also add interest for an older child. Have a drink and a snack ready at the end of the walk as a reward.

Taking your dog

Many of the walks or parts of the walks in this book are suitable for dogs. However, dogs are not allowed in national parks, which includes all of the hinterland walks. Within the Gold Coast City Council area, the restrictions can vary depending on the time of day and time of the year. Please check the local restrictions at www.goldcoast.qld.gov.au (search for "dog exercise areas") or T 1300 694 222.

There are also dog off-leash areas to enjoy adjacent to or as part of some of the walks. Remember to take along some bags to clean up after your dog, otherwise you could be fined. As the rules change from time to time be sure to check local signage.

Track closures

Tracks and paths are closed from time to time for maintenance or upgrades and to repair damage from storms, rain, floods, landslips and bushfires. Do not walk past or disregard track closure signs. Return the way you came. Often you can check closures on the website of the responsible authority.

For many of the walks in this book, track closures will be a disappointment rather

Introduction

than a problem as detours can be made. In the hinterland, track status can be found on the website www.nprsr.qld.gov.au (search for "park alerts").

Looking after the environment

All the walks in this book are on defined tracks and it is best to stay on them to avoid damaging the vegetation and creating erosion. Stick to the bushwalking code of taking nothing but photographs and leaving nothing but footprints. Take your rubbish home with you or place in bins provided. Observe the wildlife but do not disturb it. Leave cultural and heritage sites as you find them. In many areas authorities and groups of volunteers work hard to restore and maintain the environment. It is good practice to try not to make their job any harder, so ensure you do not bring unwanted plant seed into areas on dirty walking gear.

Safety

Safety plays a major part in the planning of any walk and there are a number of things to consider depending on the length and difficulty of the walk. For the longer and more remote walks in this book, be sure to look after your personal safety. Always carry your mobile phone. In a life threatening situation call 000 for assistance. If you are out of range try the mobile emergency number 112 which accesses all available networks.

Natural disasters: Natural disasters in Australia's bushland areas in recent years have claimed many lives, so pay attention and don't take unnecessary risks. The Australian bush is very susceptible to fire, so take extreme care – for example, extinguish cigarettes completely and take them away with you. At times fire bans are imposed – check the limits of bans with local authorities and do not go against them. Other possible dangers include storms, flash flooding, cyclonic weather, rough seas and floods, all of which can make walking very unsafe. Always check the weather conditions (and tide times) before heading out (see Weather, below).

Shared pathways: Many of the concrete footpaths, particularly along the foreshore, are shared with cyclists so you need to keep a careful lookout for both riders and signage indicating bike-only paths.

Weather: The weather is one of the greatest enemies of walkers. Check radio, TV, or newspapers for local weather forecasts and warnings. You can also visit the Bureau of Meteorology website at www.bom.gov.au. Avoid walking on very hot days, especially in the middle of the day (see **Protective clothing**, below).

Introduction

Cliffs: Keep well back from cliff edges and exposed areas, especially when walking with children.

Food and water: Always carry food and drinking water. You cannot rely on the water quality in creeks, streams and tanks. Allow about a litre per person for every two hours in summer and a bit less in winter. Always take some snacks. Dehydration and hunger are major causes of fatigue. If you are inexperienced, or walking with others who are less fit, a drink and snack stop always provides a chance for a rest and catch up.

Carry a First Aid kit: It's possible to buy a suitable hiking kit from an outdoor store or online from St John Ambulance Australia at www.stjohn.org.au. You can also make your own kit – there are suggestions of what to include on the St John Ambulance site.

Know your route and don't walk alone: With the possible exception of short walks in populated areas, always walk with a friend. In the more remote walks it's best to have a party of at least three people.

Protective clothing: Queensland's sun is severe, so always wear a hat and sunglasses and apply sunscreen regardless of where you are walking or the time of the year. In hot weather try to walk in the cooler parts of the day in the early morning or late afternoon, or plan to be in shady areas in the middle of the day. In hot weather the risk of heat stroke is high.

Things that bite: Whenever you walk in a bushland area, be sure to carry a good quality insect repellent.

Snakes: You are unlikely to encounter snakes but South-East Queensland does have some venomous snakes. Never let children run ahead and always have a responsible adult, who can keep an eye out for dangers, leading the walk. Most snakes prefer to avoid people and will only bite if trodden on, cornered or provoked. Stick to the path and make plenty of noise while you walk.

In the event of a bite, apply a very firm bandage from just above the fingers or toes and along the whole limb if possible. Immobilise the limb with a splint and keep the casualty calm and still. Don't cut the area or try to suck out the venom. Leave any venom on the wound as this helps in identification. Call an ambulance on 000, or the mobile emergency number 112. The St John Ambulance website has more information: www.stjohn.org.au.

Leeches and ticks: These are part of the environment in bushland areas and should be removed as soon as found. Insect repellent will help

Introduction

protect against leeches and ticks but is not always successful. Leeches will cause bleeding and their bites can become infected. Remove gently by hand or by applying insect repellent, alcohol or salt. Remove tick by spraying it with an aerosol insect repellent containing pyrethrin. Spray again one minute later. It should fall off after 24 hours. If the tick remains stuck in your skin, seek medical advice. Ticks can be dangerous as they inject toxins. Be sure to check yourself and children carefully after a day in the bush, particularly in the hair, around the head and crevices in the body. If any symptoms develop or you feel unwell, seek medical advice immediately. Ticks are very dangerous to dogs.

Swimming and sharks: The beachside walks pass many beaches patrolled by either lifeguards or volunteer lifesavers. These spots are identified by red and yellow flags. Always swim between the flags. The Surf Life Saving Australia website has more information: visit www.slsa.asn.au. Avoid swimming in canals and rivers on the Gold Coast as sharks do inhabit these waters. In rock pools take care on slippery rocks, never swim alone and supervise children and poor swimmers carefully. Be sure to follow instructions on any local signage. Always keep a watch out for others. There are a number of public swimming pools along the coast and on Tamborine Mountain.

Navigation: All the walks in this book are on paths of varying standards. In the hinterland areas you can get maps from the National Park offices, some information centres or on the website at www.nprsr.qld.gov.au.

Gold Coast Oceanway

The Gold Coast Oceanway is a 36-kilometre beachside track stretching from the Gold Coast Seaway in the north to Point Danger in the south. A number of walks (1-6 and 13, 16-19) in this book explore the Oceanway and are marked on the maps on pages iii-v. It's possible to join all of these individual tracks to create a walk which explores the entire Oceanway.

Walks at a glance

No	Walk	Page	Distance	Time
Coastal Walks: North				
1	Burleigh to Tallebudgera	14	1.2 km one way	30 mins
2	Burleigh Heads Rainforest Circuit	18	2.5 km circuit	1 hr
3	Burleigh to Nobbys Beach	22	3.5 km one way	2 hrs
4	Nobbys to Surfers Paradise	26	8 km one way	2 hrs 30 mins
5	Surfers Paradise to The Spit	32	5 km one way	2 hrs
6	Federation Walk	36	3.5 km one way	1 hr 30 mins
Beyond the Beach: North				
7	Cascade Gardens	42	2 km circuit	1 hr
8	Gold Coast Botanic Gardens	46	4 km circuit	2 hrs
9	Southport History	50	5.5 km return	2 hrs 30 mins
10	Labrador Heritage Walk	54	4.5 km circuit	2 hrs
11	Coombabah Lakelands Koala Track	58	10 km circuit	4 hrs
12	Coombabah Boardwalk	62	3 km return	1 hr
Southern Gold Coast				
13	Point Danger to Coolangatta	68	3.5 km return	2 hrs
14	Point Danger to Tweed River	72	3 km return	1 hr
15	Razorback	76	4 km return	2 hrs
16	Kirra to Currumbin	80	7 km one way	3 hrs
17	Currumbin	84	6 km return	2 hrs
18	Palm Beach	88	4 km return	1 hr 30 mins
19	Palm Beach to Tallebudgera	92	5 km one way	2 hrs
20	Tallebudgera Creek	96	3.5 km one way	1 hr 30 mins

Walks at a glance

Grade	Café	Dogs*	Swimming	Conditions	Highlights
Easy	No	No	No	Some shade	Views and surfers
Medium	Yes	No	No	Shaded	Rainforest and views
Easy/Medium	Yes	Yes	Yes	Exposed	Coastal views
Easy	Yes	Yes	Yes	Exposed	Coastal views
Easy	Yes	Yes	Yes	Exposed	Coastal Views
Easy	Yes	Yes	Yes	Exposed	Flora and fauna
Easy	No	Yes	No	Some shade	Gardens, history
Easy	No	Yes	No	Some shade	Flora
Easy	Yes	Yes	Yes	Some shade	History, views
Easy	Yes	Yes	Yes	Exposed	History, views
Easy	No	No	No	Some shade	Wildlife
Easy	No	No	No	Some shade	Flora and fauna
Easy	Yes	Yes	Yes	Mostly exposed	Beach views
Easy	Yes	Yes	Yes	Mostly exposed	Beach views
Medium	No	No	No	Mostly exposed	Views
Easy	Yes	Yes	Yes	Mostly exposed	Views, history
Easy	Yes	Yes	Yes	Mostly exposed	Views and public art
Easy	Yes	Yes	Yes	Mostly exposed	Creek views
Easy	Yes	Yes	Yes	Exposed	Coastal Views
Easy	No	Yes	Yes	Mostly exposed	Creek views

Walks at a glance

No	Walk	Page	Distance	Time
Hinterland North: Tamborine				
21	Cedar Creek Falls	102	1 km return	30 mins
22	Jenyns Circuit	106	5 km circuit	2 hrs
23	Cameron Falls and Sandy Creek	110	2.5 km circuit	1 hr
24	MacDonald Rainforest Circuit	114	1.5 km circuit	30 mins
25	Witches Falls Circuit	118	3 km circuit	1 hr
26	Witches Chase	122	5.5 km circuit	2 hrs
27	Curtis Falls	126	3.5 km return	1 hr 30 mins
Hinterland South: Springbrook				
28	Springbrook Warrie Circuit	132	17 km circuit	6 hrs
29	Twin Falls Circuit	136	4 km circuit	2 hrs
30	Purling Brook Falls	140	4 km circuit	2 hrs
31	Apple Tree park to Settlement Day Use Area	144	7 km one way	3 hrs
32	Natural Bridge	148	1 km circuit	1 hr
33	Mount Cougal Cascades	152	1.5 km return	1 hr

* Dogs are not allowed in National Parks at all. Within the Gold Coast City Council area, restrictions can vary with time of day and time of the year. Please check local signage or call the council on 1300 694 222.

Walks at a glance

Grade	Café	Dogs*	Swimming	Conditions	Highlights
Medium	No	No	No	Partly shaded	Creek views and falls
Medium	No	No	No	Shady	Rainforest and views
Medium	No	No	No	Shady	Views and rainforest
Easy	No	No	No	Shady	Rainforest
Medium	No	No	No	Some shade	Rainforest and views
Medium	No	No	No	Some shade	Rainforest and views
Medium	Yes	No	No	Shady	Waterfall and rainforest
Hard	No	No	No	Partly shaded	Rainforest, waterfalls
Medium	Yes	No	No	Shaded	Waterfalls
Medium	No	No	No	Shaded	Waterfalls and views
Hard	No	No	No	Shaded	Waterfalls
Easy	No	No	No	Shaded	Rock formation
Easy	No	No	Yes	Shady	Cascades, history

Coastal Walks North

The northern end of the Gold Coast offers the bustle of the entertainment and tourist district as well as pockets of natural bushland, rare coastal rainforest and oceanside parks which run along the area's golden beaches. The walks in this section explore the coastal strip between Burleigh and The Spit, and its landscaped esplanades with picnic facilities, playgrounds and magnificent views along the coast. The Gold Coast is famous for its tall buildings behind the beach and one walk takes you past the Coast's earliest example of high-rise architecture as well as one of the world's tallest residential buildings. Some of these walks are suitable as evening strolls as they are along well-lit paths.

Board riders at Burleigh

1 Burleigh to Tallebudgera

Burleigh Heads, originally named Burly Head in 1840, is one of the few headlands along the Gold Coast's strip of sandy beaches. As the Gold Coast's only coastal National Park (proclaimed in 1886), it provides an opportunity for two walks in the tranquillity of the forest. This coastal walk is the easier of the two, and takes you around the lower edge of the Park with views from the point along the coast.

At a glance

Grade: Easy
Time: 30 mins
Distance: 1.2 km one way
Conditions: Some shade, sealed track

Getting there:

Bus: Check www.translink.com.au or T 13 12 30 for buses from your location

Car: Travel along the Gold Coast Highway to Burleigh Heads and near the Surf Club turn into Goodwin Terrace which runs parallel to the beach and uphill towards the headland. There is street parking in Goodwin Terrace

View to Surfers Paradise

1 Burleigh to Tallebudgera

Walk directions

1 Start on the northern side, at the end of Goodwin Terrace (which runs along the beachfront). Take the lower, sealed track, which goes off to the left. You're likely to be sharing this path with surfers carrying boards in search of waves off the point.

2 Along the way are several side tracks down to the rocky foreshore. It's possible to explore these tracks, but be very careful as the rocks are slippery and large waves are unpredictable. The rocks and headland are composed of basalt, a volcanic rock. This is a good spot for scenic views and birdwatching, and there are some good examples of the pandanus palm, which can survive in harsh coastal conditions.

3 About 120 metres along the track is a gate and a warning sign that you are entering a rock fall area. Continue walking for about 250 metres to the other side of the rock fall area. However, do not continue in wet weather or if the gate is closed.

4 The vegetation now opens out into grassy slopes and coastal heath. High above are some examples of the six-sided columnar basalt formations that make up the headland and descend to form the rocky foreshore. The basalt was formed from the volcanic lava flows of Mt Warning some 23 million years ago.

5 As the vegetation changes again, from coastal heath to rainforest, there are views through the forest to Point Danger, away to the south. Closer by is the breakwater at the mouth of Tallebudgera Creek, a popular recreation area.

Basalt columns

Tallebudgera Creek

15

1 Burleigh to Tallebudgera

Bush turkey

6 Half a kilometre from the gate mentioned at waypoint 3 is a second gate. From here there are sidetracks to the sandy beaches on the northern side of Tallebudgera Creek. Continue on the main track.

7 When you reach a fork in the track, take the path to the left. Near this intersection is a sign explaining the legend of Gowonda the Hunter, a traditional dreamtime story of the local Indigenous people, the Kombumerri.

8 A little further on is Echo Beach, a seagrass habitat. All of these sandy beaches are popular fishing spots and at the western end of this beach is a wheelchair and stroller accessible fishing platform. Swimming is not recommended in this area as there are dangerous currents.

9 You'll soon reach the southern entrance to the track, marked *Burleigh Head National Park*. From here you can turn right and follow the highway for 100 metres to an interesting information centre which has displays about the local area. Alternatively, on the southern side of Tallebudgera Creek is a swimming area that often has lifesavers on patrol. Bathe only where you see the red and yellow flags. For the return trip there are several options. You can retrace your steps back to the beginning, return via Walk 2 through the rainforest, or catch a bus (routes 700, 702, 706, 765) back to Burleigh.

1 Burleigh to Tallebudgera

Gold Coast environment – Pandanus palm

Pandanus tectorius, also known as the coastal screw palm or pandanus palm, is a native of the area. It's usually found in exposed positions, its array of propping roots holding onto rocky foreshores or sandy beaches. The fruits are oval shaped, and often as large as a football. The segments of the fruit turn orange-red when ripe and fall separately. The fruit was roasted and the seeds eaten by the local Indigenous peoples. In other parts of Queensland, there are records of parts of the tree being used to make dilly bags, baskets and rafts. You should not eat the fruit. As this area is part of a National Park you are not allowed to remove any seeds, fruit, flowers or vegetation.

Pandanas palm

2 Burleigh Heads Rainforest Circuit

You'll be rewarded with sweeping views on this energetic walk through Burleigh Headland National Park. The track takes you over the top and around the headland, through rare coastal rainforest. Along the way, lookouts offer views of the skyscrapers of Surfers Paradise and, on a clear day, you can see beyond Surfers Paradise to Stradbroke Island and south to Point Danger on the Queensland-New South Wales border.

Tallebudgera Creek, looking south

At a glance

Grade: Medium
Time: 1 hr
Distance: 2.5 km circuit
Conditions: Shaded

Getting there:

Bus: Check www.translink.com.au or T 13 12 30 for buses from your location

Car: Travel along the Gold Coast Highway to Burleigh Heads and near the Surf Club turn into Goodwin Terrace which runs parallel to the beach and uphill towards the headland. There is street parking in Goodwin Terrace

2 Burleigh Heads Rainforest Circuit

Walk directions

1 Start on the northern side at the end of Goodwin Terrace, which runs along the beachfront from the patrolled surf beach. Take the upper track that goes off to your right and heads uphill. Very soon you climb some steps, about ninety in total.

2 Look out for bush turkey nests on the ground in this area. The birds make large heaps from forest floor litter and the heat caused by decaying leaves incubates the eggs buried inside. Bush turkeys are one of the most prominent forms of wildlife remaining in the forest. From here the track zigzags uphill. Watch the rocks and soils as you go and you can see the deeply weathered sediments. These form the lower areas of the headland.

3 After about 250 metres take a short track to the left. This leads to a lookout with views to the north towards Surfers Paradise. On a clear day you can see to Stradbroke Island, defined by the massive exposed sand hills

Burleigh Rainforest

2 Burleigh Heads Rainforest Circuit

in the far distance. Return to the main track and here the dark volcanic basalt rocks that cap the headland can soon be seen. Continue on uphill.

4 After another 300 metres, at a fork in the track, take the right-hand path that now starts to go downhill. You'll return to this spot on the walk later. Along the track are glimpses of urban development in the area and views to the ranges west of the Gold Coast. There is a diverse range of vegetation in the forest here and you're likely to hear and see bird life as you walk downhill.

5 Another track, leading to Tallebudgera Creek and the Ocean View Track (Walk 1), joins on the right-hand side after 600 metres. Don't take this path, however, but continue on as the track begins a steady uphill climb for a further 600 metres, with views through the rainforest to Tallebudgera Creek and to the south.

National Park entrance

20

2 Burleigh Heads Rainforest Circuit

6 At the top is Tumgun Lookout. From here there are views to the south all the way to Point Danger. In whale-watching season, during the cooler months, you can sometimes see whales as they breach and blow on their migration along the coast. Also look out for some of the larger coastal seabirds such as kites and osprey. Continue following the track downhill for 160 metres. When you reach a junction (waypoint 4), turn right. Now you are back on the earlier part of the track heading downhill. Retrace your steps, passing waypoints 3 and 2, and so finally returning to your starting point.

Surfers Paradise

Out and about – Whale-watching

Lookouts along the coast provide a good opportunity for whale-watching, with the best time being from May to November. Later in the season there is a chance of seeing mothers with their newborn calves heading south again. The whales often cruise within a few kilometres of the beach so a pair of binoculars will allow you to see their breaching and tail-waving performances and blows. While the mornings are usually calmer, the afternoons can be spectacular from mainland vantage points as the sun highlights the whales' performances. The magnificent humpback whale (*Megaptera novaeangliae*) is one of the world's largest mammals, measuring sixteen metres or more in length and weighing in at 40 tonnes. They migrate north early in the season, often returning south in July or August. A famous visitor to our shores is the albino humpback whale Migaloo, first sighted in 1991 and eagerly awaited each year. Also keep an eye out for bottlenose dolphins (*Tursiops truncatus*), often seen playing close to shore and riding the waves.

3 Burleigh to Nobbys Beach

Most of this walk is on a wide, flat concrete track, although there is a climb over South Nobby Hill at about the halfway point, followed by steps down to Miami Beach. The short climb to South Nobby headland is rewarded with views right along the coast.

Burleigh Beach

At a glance

Grade: Easy/Medium
Time: 2 hrs
Distance: 3.5 km one way
Conditions: Exposed, some shade

Getting there:

Bus: Check www.translink.com.au or T 13 12 30 for buses from your location

Car: Travel along the Gold Coast Highway to Burleigh Heads, turning on to The Esplanade where there is street parking. From the Gold Coast Highway at Miami turn into Santa Monica Av on the southern side of the Miami High School and follow to Marine Parade where there is street parking

3 Burleigh to Nobbys Beach

Walk directions

1 Begin at the beach area adjacent to the Burleigh Surf Club at the intersection of the Gold Coast Highway and Goodwin Terrace. With the ocean on your right, head north on the concrete path towards the distant high-rise buildings of Surfers Paradise. Take care as this is a shared path with cyclists. At dusk, in the trees along the start of the track, you'll hear the noisy chatter of scaly-breasted lorikeets and their more colourful cousins, rainbow lorikeets. There is a fitness course in the beachside parklands, with description of the exercises that can be performed on a variety of obstacles. For the younger ones, there are several playgrounds.

2 Look out for a bright yellow lifeguard tower and a patrolled surfing beach. This is the halfway point to North Burleigh. You may hear or see birdlife in the bush inside the fenced area to the right. This area is fenced to protect the dunes – establishing the vegetation helps to stabilise the sand.

3 At North Burleigh, pass in front of the North Burleigh SLSC. The Club welcomes visitors and has refreshments available all day. Just past the club is Ed Hardy Park. A plaque here tells you of the community contributions made by Ed Hardy and his involvement in establishing the club.

4 A few hundred metres further on is a park named after Mick Schamburg, who was the parks and gardens supervisor for the Gold Coast City Council from 1950–1975. A plaque provides more details. From here continue up the bitumen path to the top of South Nobby Headland where there are good views to the north and south.

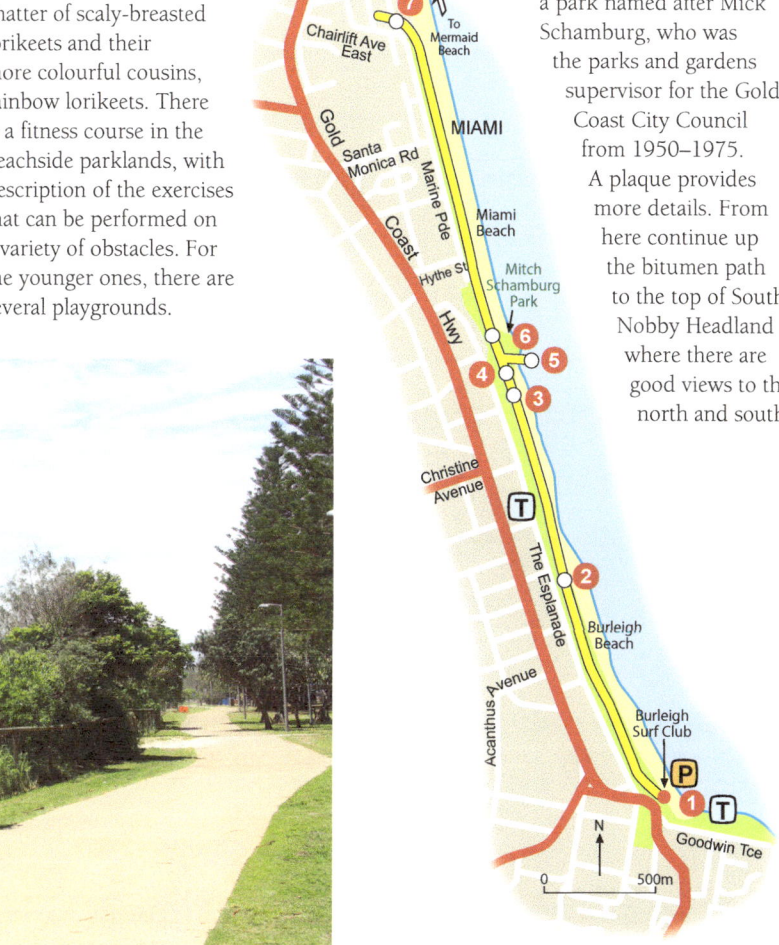

3 Burleigh to Nobbys Beach

5 At the fork in the track take the short side trip to the right to the wooden verandah lookout for views to the north. A little further along is another wooden deck with views to the south, back along the way you have come. The building adjacent to this lookout is the Gold Coast Surf Rescue Communications Centre. Retrace your steps to the main track and follow it along the fenced cliff top. There are a few seats here, so it is a good spot for a rest.

6 You'll soon reach a narrow set of ninety steps. Follow these down to Miami Beach. Pass through the park area and, with the beach on your right, pass the caravan park on the left. Just ahead is the Miami SLSC which has a street level coffee shop. From here the track is exposed and follows the beachfront for another kilometre. Again there are picnic facilities and a playground. Keep an eye out for the seats and tables in this area which have been designed and built in the shape of surfboards.

7 Finish the walk where the beachfront path finishes, near the intersection of Marine Parade and Chairlift Avenue East. If you wish to retrace your steps back to the starting point, you'll find numerous facilities for refreshments to meet most budgets in Burleigh. Alternatively, walk a little way up Chairlift Ave, then right into Seagull Ave and left into Lavarack Road. Turn right at the end to find a bus stop. Buses from here will take you back very close to your start point. Check Translink for times.

3 Burleigh to Nobbys Beach

Walk variation

This walk can be started from either end and made shorter by choosing an earlier spot to turn around. Variety can be added by choosing to walk along the beach for some sections. To cross the headland you will have to use the track, as the surf comes right up to the rocks, which can be very slippery and dangerous.

Burleigh Foreshore

Out and about – Beachfront markets

There is a range of art, craft and food markets throughout the Gold Coast. The parks along the beachfront come alive with markets regularly on Sundays to a set timetable. These are great places for locally made souvenirs and gifts ranging from the traditional to the quirky. There are also food stalls where you can snack or buy something to take away for later. Markets are held on the first and third Sunday of each month at Broadbeach in Kurrawa Park, the second Sunday at Coolangatta along Marine Parade and on the last Sunday at Burleigh Heads on The Esplanade. As dates may change, check the market calendar for up-to-date news (www.artandcraft.com.au).

4 Nobbys Beach to Surfers Paradise

Beginning in parklands near Nobbys Hill and finishing in the bustling centre of Surfers Paradise, this walk takes you past one of the world's tallest residential buildings. You can walk all, or part of the way on the beach and there are many spots to stop for a break, a coffee or a swim at a patrolled surfing beach.

At a glance
Grade: Easy
Time: 2 hrs 30 mins
Distance: 8 km one way
Conditions: Exposed

Getting there:
Bus: Check www.translink.com.au or T 13 12 30 for buses from your location

Car: From the Gold Coast Highway at Miami turn into Santa Monica Av on the southern side of the Miami High School and follow to Marine Parade where there is street parking

4 Nobbys Beach to Surfers Paradise

Walk directions

1 Start at the end of the parklands at the northern end of Marine Parade, near Chairlift Avenue East. Follow the footpath as it leads away from the beach, into Albatross Avenue, and shortly to Nobbys Beach SLSC, established in 1954. Continue along Albatross Avenue on the sealed footpath that is sheltered from the beach by housing, built in a diversity of styles.

2 Four blocks on at Seashell Avenue, the road has a slight kink as it becomes Hedges Avenue. The beachfront houses here are among the most expensive in the area. Continue along this narrow, one-way road.

3 Pass the Mermaid Beach SLSC (established in 1945) and continue following the footpath.

4 After a little over a kilometre, the housing gives way to parklands and the path moves away from the road. These parks have wide open spaces with picnic shelters, BBQs, toilets and changing facilities. There are also children's playgrounds with some fenced enclosures. Along the beachfront are revegetation reserves, which often contain interesting birdlife. The area has both dog on- and off-leash areas. There are also exercise trails and equipment. A common tree in beachside reserves is the she-oak, which has needle-like leaves.

5 Less than a kilometre further on you'll reach Kurrawa Beach, and the Kurrawa SLSC, established in 1958. In front of the club is the Robert Gatenby Boardwalk, constructed in memory of Robert who, at 15, lost his life in Kurrawa's under-18 boat crew at the 1996 Australia Surf Life Saving titles. Across the road is the Oasis shopping centre and the site of the former Lennons Broadbeach Hotel, which opened in 1955. It was built at a cost of £550,000 ($1,100,000) and is considered one of the first high-rise buildings on the coast.

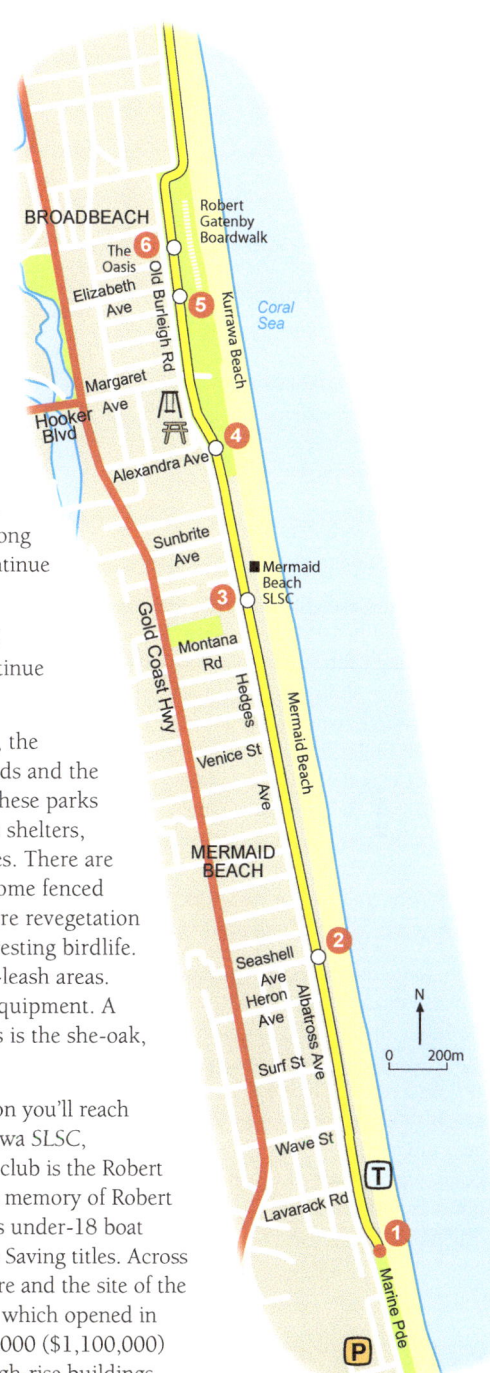

4 Nobbys Beach to Surfers Paradise

6 Continue on the path to Paula Stafford Park, which commemorates the clothing designer responsible for bringing the bikini to the coast in 1952. At the time, this two-piece swimsuit was considered quite shocking and the model who wore the first bikini was ordered off the beach. Close by is a park dedicated to Lorraine Stumm Palmer, a distinguished journalist and war correspondent. Many of the parks along this walk are named after local people and you'll find plaques with details of their achievements.

7 Pass the Broadbeach SLSC, which opened in 1935. Behind this is the Bowling Club and across the road is a local coffee shop. Further on is Geoffrey Cornish Walk named after a former Bomber Command pilot in World War II who later, as a doctor, settled on the coast and had great success helping heart patients with exercise programs. Along the way are she-oaks and pandanus palms. This section of the beachfront comes alive with a local market on the first Sunday morning of the month.

8 Towards the end of the parklands is Graeme Brien Park. Graeme was executive director of the Queensland Cancer Fund which, under his leadership, became very successful. The track now leaves the beachfront, turning into First Avenue. At the next intersection turn right into Old Burleigh Road. As you walk along the road the buildings get taller and there are fewer of the original beach houses.

Walk variations

You may choose to walk some sections along the beach. The SLSCs and lifeguard towers provide good navigation points.

4 Nobbys Beach to Surfers Paradise

Pandanas palm

Q1 building

29

4 Nobbys Beach to Surfers Paradise

9 At the end of Old Burleigh Road turn right into Fern Street then left into Garfield Terrace. Pass by Northcliffe SLSC, established in 1947. Along the skyline you can see Q1, one of the world's tallest residential buildings. If you'd like a closer look, five streets further on is Hamilton Avenue which takes you to the door of Q1. Otherwise continue straight on along Northcliffe Terrace.

10 At Hanlan Street, turn left. About halfway along this short street is the heritage-listed Kinkabool Apartments, Surfers Paradise's first high-rise building, although it is now dwarfed by taller buildings. Take the first right into Surfers Paradise Boulevard.

11 Take the first right into Cavill Avenue, often regarded as the centre of Surfers Paradise. On this corner once stood the Surfers Paradise Hotel, which was destroyed by fire in 1936, rebuilt in 1937 and finally demolished in 1983. Just behind the hotel was the Surfers Paradise Zoo, which closed in 1957. Walk down the Mall, first built in 1976, to the beachfront. It was here in 1966, that a World War II German mine washed ashore and was destroyed by the Navy. This is the end of the walk. To return to the start via public transport, first jump on the tram at the junction of Caville Ave and Surfers Paradise Boulevard (heading south). At Broadbeach South Station get off the tram and catch a southern bound bus - get off just before Lavarack Road. Check Translink for times.

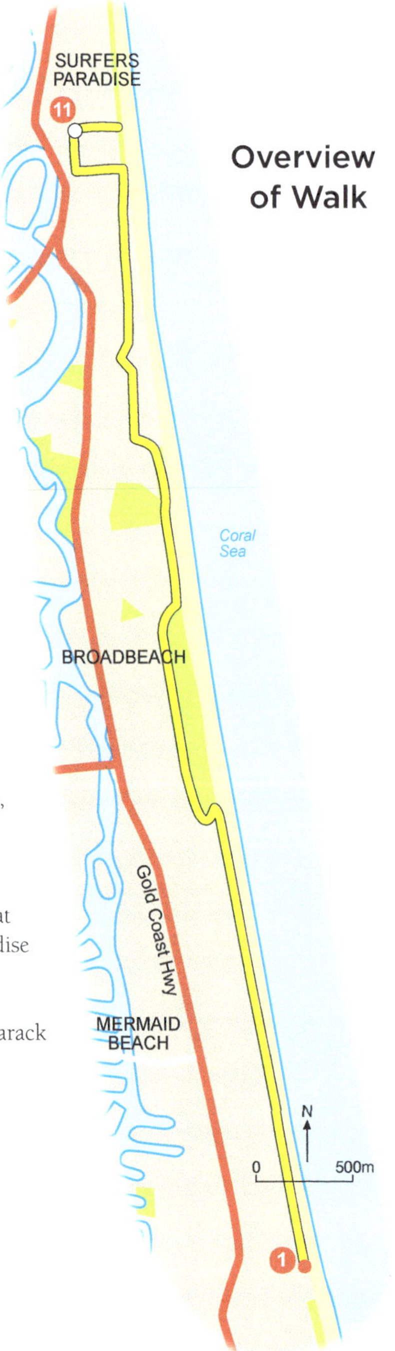

Overview of Walk

4 Nobbys Beach to Surfers Paradise

Gold Coast history – Those high-rise buildings

Today, the Gold Coast is known for its high-rise buildings, but it had a very different skyline back in 1956 when the five-storey Lennons Broadbeach Hotel was the Gold Coast's tallest building. Most visitors to the Coast camped or stayed in caravans or low-rise boarding houses. However, heritage-listed Kinkabool Apartments at Surfers Paradise, just south of Cavill Avenue, marked the beginning of Gold Coast high-rise architecture, reaching 10 storeys – or 27 metres – when it was completed in 1960. Since then, the skyline has continued to grow, with the first buildings to reach 20 storeys appearing in 1971. Today, Q1 is one of the world's tallest residential buildings at 80 storeys. You can visit its observation deck on level 77 for 360° views over the coast and the hinterland. The many cranes on the Gold Coast skyline are testimony that more high-rises are on the way.

Kinkabool Apartments

5 Surfers Paradise to The Spit

Bustling Cavill Mall marks the beginning of this walk, which follows the beachfront on a wide sealed pathway and ends near Sea World on The Spit. The walk passes through parklands at Narrow Neck, where the Nerang River and the ocean almost meet. There are plenty of opportunities on the way to watch surfers, swim at a patrolled beach or stop at a café.

At a glance

Grade: Easy
Time: 2 hrs
Distance: 5 km one way
Conditions: Exposed

Getting there:

Bus: Check www.translink.com.au or T 13 12 30 for buses from your location

Car: From the Gold Coast Highway take Elkhorn Av towards the beachfront, where there is metered parking on the Esplanade

Southport Broadwater

5 Surfers Paradise to The Spit

Walk directions

1 Start on the beachfront path, at the end of Cavill Mall. Facing the ocean, turn left and head north, following the wide, sealed pathway. On this section of the walk you'll pass by landscaped parklands, public exercise equipment and plenty of picnic and toilet facilities. Trees lining the path are pandanus palms, and she-oaks, which have needle-like leaves. Watch the path for markers to show which side to walk on. There are coffee shops across the road.

2 After a while the path enters a bushy area and passes a lifeguard centre before emerging onto the roadside at Narrow Neck, an area popular with board riders and kite surfers. Look out for a cairn with pointers to features in the distance, such as Point Danger, Stradbroke Island and Lamington National Park.

3 A little further on, on the other side of the road, is a prominent bridge. You could take a detour here to explore MacIntosh Island Park. Otherwise continue following the beachside footpath.

4 After about 600 metres, opposite John Kemp Street, the track turns right into the parklands. Look out for the sculpture called "Melody". Continue following the path as it passes through beachside vegetation, which plays an important role in stabilising the sand.

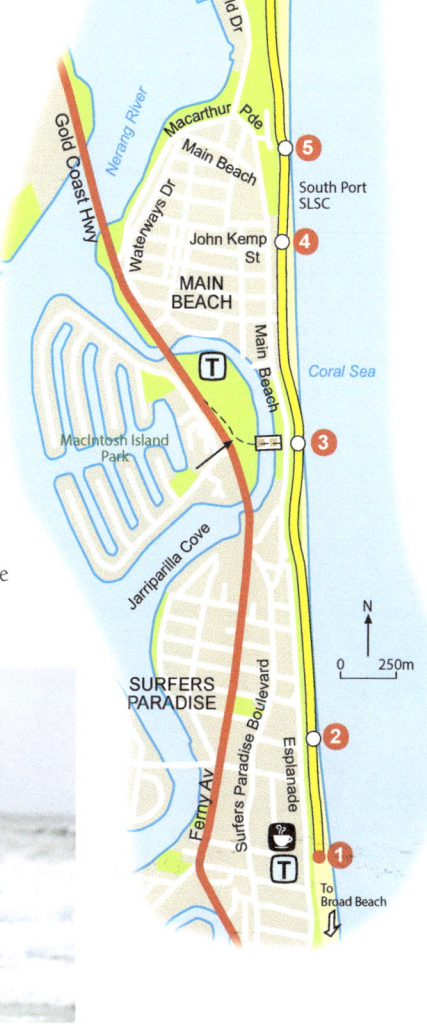

33

5 Surfers Paradise to The Spit

5 Pass the Main Beach SLSC and, shortly after, an Oceanway Walk marker that shows distances to various spots.

6 The track passes between the beach and Sheraton Mirage Resort. Along this section, stay on the main track as the side paths to the left go to Seaworld Drive and the resorts. This area was once extensively mined for mineral sands, but it has since been restored and revegetated.

7 The path becomes loose gravel and shortly you arrive at signpost near Lifeguard Tower 42. Take the turn towards Sea World and the car park. This is the end of the walk and there are picnic and toilet facilities here and a bus stop nearby.

34

5 Surfers Paradise to The Spit

Walk variation

Walk back to Main Beach via Seaworld Drive. You'll pass by the Gold Coast Fishermen's Co-operative, where from 7am daily you can buy fresh seafood directly from the person who caught it. Visitors can get access to the fishing boats via floating pontoons. The catch includes fish, crabs, bugs and prawns.

Gold Coast history – Meter Maids

In the mid-1960s, parking meters were installed in Surfers Paradise with a $2 fine for motorists who overparked. Local identity and businessman Bernie Elsey started the Meter Maids service in response to local business' fears that the meters, also called 'kerbside bandits', would damage trade. The Maids were dressed in gold bikinis and tiaras and wandered the street feeding expired parking meters and leaving a card under the windscreen wipers. While controversial at the time, many years later in 1967 the Gold Coast Mayor Sir Bruce Small took the Meter Maids on a promotional tour to get people back to the Gold Coast beaches after they had been ravaged by cyclonic seas. This idea took off with worldwide publicity. Today the Meter Maids are still at work in Surfers Paradise with the tiaras replaced by Akubra hats.

6 Federation Walk

The narrow strip of sand separating the Nerang River estuary from the ocean is known as The Spit. It's home to Sea World and a number of luxury resorts, but also has walking tracks that explore the coastal sand dunes. Community groups, including Friends of Federation Walk, are helping to revegetate this unique coastal habitat. This walk was established to commemorate the 2001 Centenary of Federation.

At a glance

Grade: Easy
Time: 1 hr 30 mins
Distance: 3.5 km one way
Conditions: Exposed

Getting there:

Bus: Check www.translink.com.au or T 13 12 30 for buses from your location

Car: From Main Beach follow Seaworld Drive for about 1.5 km to the car park opposite Sea World entrance

Flowering Wattle

6 Federation Walk

Walk directions

1 Begin at the car park on the opposite side of the road from Sea World. On the northern side of the car park, find an information board with details on the Friends of Federation Walk. This marks the beginning of the walk.

2 After a short distance you'll find a plaque giving details of this community project. When the first section of the walk was officially opened in January 2001, over 5000 people attended the ceremony and school children planted more than 100 trees. Continue following the track, which is lined by logs.

3 You'll soon reach an area which is being revegetated; stakes marked with coloured tags support the new plants. On the last Sunday of each month, visitors are welcome to participate in community planting days. Visit www.federationwalk.org for details. Ignore the numerous side tracks that lead either to car parks along Seaworld Drive or to the ocean beach. Keep an eye out for small, colourful birds and butterflies. Even if you do not see the birds they can be heard as they sing in the surrounding vegetation.

6 Federation Walk

4 The path emerges into open country and is crossed by tracks to the beach and road. Ignore these and continue on the main path.

5 A little further on is an area where the track goes to Lifeguard Tower 45, and there is a sign indicating the underground high voltage cables providing power to the Southport Seaway. Continue on the main track and you'll soon reach a fenced area enclosing a weather recording station, which the track skirts round.

6 Straight ahead is the Gold Coast Seaway Sand Bypass Jetty. Walk under the jetty, but be careful as there is low head clearance. To the left, towards the start of the jetty, is a sign explaining its operations. The track to the right leads to a popular surfing beach. Continue on the main track for 300 metres.

7 When you reach a bitumen path, turn right and walk out to the end of the Southport Seaway for views along the coast. This is the turnaround point of this walk. To visit a café, retrace your steps along the bitumen path, going 100 metres past waypoint 7 to the Volunteer Marine Rescue station. Beyond is a car park and the Seaway Café. Return to the beginning of the walk via the same track.

Superb Fairy-Wren

Track to the Spit

Walk variation

Rather than returning via the same track, you could pick up the Oceanway Walk (see map on page 37) that runs closer to the ocean beach. It will bring you back to the start near Lifeguard Tower 42. Another option is to walk one-way along the ocean beach. This is best done at low tide when the sand is hard.

6 Federation Walk

Sand Bypass Jetty

Gold Coast environment – Gold Coast Seaway and Sand Bypass Jetty

The area between The Spit and South Stradbroke Island was known as the Southport Bar. The bar was often dangerous, and being the main entrance from the Pacific Ocean into the Southport Broadwater and the Nerang River, a safer passage was required. Two rock walls were built to stabilise the entrance and this became known as the Southport Seaway when it was opened in 1986.

The Sand Bypass Jetty, which is almost 500 metres long, is a popular recreation spot, but has a more functional purpose. The Spit was formed by the northerly drifting sand along the coast and with the construction of the Seaway sand was trapped by the retaining wall. The jetty has a series of jet pumps and pipes that move sand from the seabed to shore. The water and sand slurry is pumped under the seaway for one and a half kilometres onto the ocean beach of South Stradbroke Island. This was the world's first permanent sand bypass operation and replaces more expensive dredging.

Coombabah Lake

Beyond The Beach – North

Behind the famous golden beaches and high-rise buildings of the Gold Coast there is another world. Just a short drive away are parks, gardens and conservation reserves. These are places for a quiet stroll, a walk with your four-legged friend or a picnic in a shady spot when you tire of the sun and surf. Walkers interested in local history will find reminders of the past and of those who pioneered the area.

Here you can explore what it was like before the time of cars, and before bridges allowed easy access to the surf beaches. Nature lovers will find a surprisingly wide range of plant species flourishing in areas not too far from the busy streets of Surfers Paradise – remember to keep your eye out for koalas and wallabies.

7 Cascade Gardens

Right next to the Gold Coast Convention Centre on the Gold Coast Highway is a little patch of bush and parklands. Though small, there's a lot to explore including a rainforest area, waterbird habitat, Korean War memorial and Kokoda Memorial. There's also a large open playground, a picnic space, views along the Nerang River and information about the local Indigenous community. The Gardens are open 6 am to 6 pm daily.

At a glance

Grade: Easy
Time: 1 hr
Distance: 2 km circuit
Conditions: Some shade

Getting there

Bus: Bus stop near main entrance; T 13 12 30 for timetable information

Car: Drive to 2730 Gold Coast Highway, Broadbeach. Parking at main entrance and on internal circuit road

Nerang River

7 Cascade Gardens

Walk directions

1 Begin at the entrance to the Cascade Gardens area adjacent to the car park, where there is a map of the grounds and information about the area. The central section of the Gardens is Rotary Park. To the left is the start of the Kokoda Track Memorial Walk. Here a plaque explains the significance of the Kokoda Track to Australians during World War II. The track was built to commemorate the sixtieth anniversary of the campaign and to provide visitors with an insight into the conditions endured by the men and women who fought in that campaign.

2 Find the nearby relief map of the Kokoda Track which gives an indication of the rugged nature of its terrain and very difficult conditions along the almost one hundred kilometres of the famous hike. The tropical rainforest here has been created to simulate the conditions in New Guinea, and at intervals there are plaques with details of the site and battles along the Kokoda Track. These are similar to the plaques along the actual Kokoda Track. Just after the relief map, follow the track leading to the left. After several hundred metres, you'll turn and begin following the riverbank.

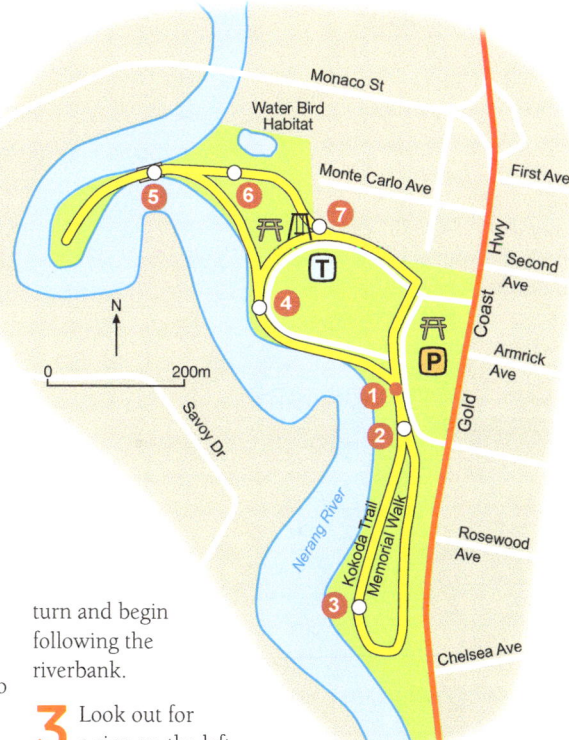

3 Look out for a sign on the left which gives details of the Cascade Gardens flying fox colony. They are the noisy animals you can hear up in the trees. The flying fox is becoming rare and the Cascade Gardens is an important flying fox sanctuary. These flying native mammals perform important work pollinating some species of tree and spreading the seed of others. The circuit brings you back to waypoint 2. From here turn left on the road, following the river.

4 You'll soon be able to join a walking path which follows the water and turns gently to the left. There are plenty of shady picnic facilities in this area.

5 Cross the gravel-covered bridge and find your way out to explore the point beyond, where you'll have views of the water and the houses on the far side. In this area you'll see mangrove trees which are tolerant of salty water. There are also she-oaks which have needle-like leaves. Retrace your steps to the open parkland.

6 You'll see a fenced waterbird habitat with a variety of birds including ducks and waterhens. Walk past the covered playground on your right. When you reach the road, turn left and walk through the parkland.

43

7 Cascade Gardens

7 When you reach a picnic and BBQ area, you'll find a memorial garden in honour of two firefighters who lost their lives fighting a fire at Southport. Follow the road back to the car park and your starting point. You may like to explore the other features, memorials and facilities of the Cascade Gardens.

Pacific Black Duck

Australian history – Kokoda

The Kokoda Track in Papua New Guinea has become a symbol of Australia's role in World War II much as Gallipoli has for World War I. The track stretches for 96 kilometres and was the scene of bloody battles between the Allied, mostly Australian, forces and the Japanese Army. This is believed to have been the turning point in the war against the advancing Japanese Army in 1942. The battles were fought in the Owen Stanley Ranges which are home to some of the roughest, most isolated and dense forest in the world. The area was only accessible on foot. Troops walked on tracks that rose to over 2000 metres, and at that altitude, while the days were hot and steamy, the nights could be cold. They endured never-ending mud and tropical diseases. The stories of survival and courage of both the troops and the local villagers is legendary. Today the track from the coast to the village of Kokoda is a gruelling overland trek but is popular with walkers keen to experience something of Australia's history.

7 Cascade Gardens

Gold Coast environment – Flying fox

Flying foxes play an important role in pollinating the flowers of forest trees and spreading seed to ensure the survival of the forest. However, they are becoming rare on the Gold Coast due to land clearing for development. There are flying fox colonies in several areas of bushland, sometimes very close to housing areas. They are noisy and have a distinctive smell. Normally you will see them resting high up in trees during the day and flying off at sunset to search for food. You should not approach or touch a flying fox as a small number are infected with the potentially deadly lyssavirus. If bitten or scratched see a doctor immediately. If you find an injured flying fox, call the RSPCA (T (07) 3426 9999) who will put you in touch with a person trained to handle flying foxes.

45

8 Gold Coast Botanic Gardens Circuit

This is the place for anyone who'd like to learn more about the plants of the Gold Coast as the walking paths take you past educational displays. The gardens are also the perfect spot for a relaxing walk and to admire the wonderful array of vegetation. There are walking paths, boardwalks and dog on/off leash areas within these 30 hectares of gardens, just ten minutes from Surfers Paradise. The Gardens are open every day from dawn to dusk.

At a glance

Grade: Easy
Time: 2 hrs
Distance: 4 km circuit
Conditions: Some shade
Dogs: Yes in some areas. Dog off-leash area.

Getting There

Bus: Gold Coast buses along Ashmore Road, T 13 12 30

Car: Drive to 232 Ashmore Road, Benowa, opposite Benowa State High School. Parking in the Gardens

Botanic Gardens

8 Gold Coast Botanic Gardens Circuit

Walk directions

1 Begin at the Friends' Centre and follow the road towards the boardwalk on the lagoon. (This is a dog 'no-go' zone.) Pick up the walking track and, keeping the water on your right, follow the path beside the lake. Join the boardwalk and at the fork in the boardwalk go left and join the walking path.

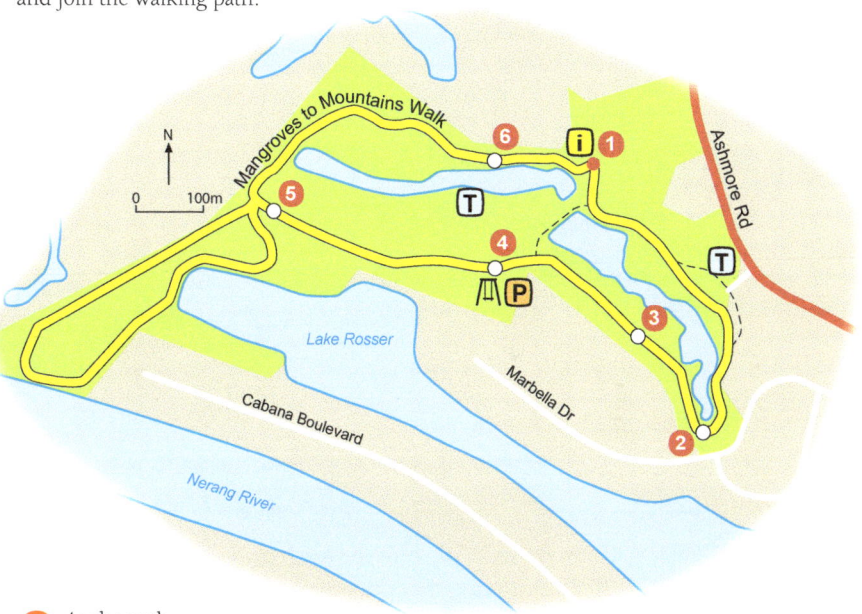

2 As the path turns, you'll find the Myrtaceae Garden. Look out for a sign which explains the major Australian plant group *Myrtaceae* which includes eucalypts (including gum trees), tea-trees and bottlebrushes. There are also a number of sculptures of Australian animals here, such as the kangaroo, koala, emu, wombat and pelican.

3 You'll soon reach the Sensory Garden which was built by the Gold Coast City Council and the Rotary service club to celebrate the centenary of Rotary in 2003. Here you will find four audio displays which take you on a tour through the senses of sight, touch, smell and sound in the gardens. 100 metres further on are the Display Gardens. Continue on the main path and follow it as it crosses the bitumen road.

4 Pass the children's playground and car park. If you have a dog, there is a dog leash area just ahead.

5 At a fork in the path, go left, then left again. Follow the one-kilometre circuit around. In the corner is a large fig tree after which Fig Tree Lawn is named. Keep an eye out here for some of the wide variety of birdlife to be found in the gardens. After returning to waypoint 5, turn left and follow the path which soon curves to the right.

6 Pass by the *Mangroves to Mountain* sign. Mangroves play a very important part in the life cycle of many fish species, providing a sheltering 'nursery' area. They've also been described as 'coastal kidneys' because they filter out sediment from run-off

8 Gold Coast Botanic Gardens Circuit

Sensory garden

water before it flows into the ocean. The oldest known mangrove tree is over 730 years old. You might like to take a small detour to explore this path, otherwise continue on for a short distance to return to the Friends' Centre and the beginning of the walk.

Sensory Garden

The audio displays in the Sensory Garden are each located close to a garden bed where the plants show the distinctive features of that particular sense. The displays are operated by push button and operate for a minute or two. The four different senses illustrated are: sight, with the marvels of colours and form; touch, with different leaf shapes and surfaces as well as spines, thorns and hairs; smell, with different perfumes of flowers and finally sound, with the noise of the wind, water and birds in the garden.

8 Gold Coast Botanic Gardens Circuit

Australian environment – Myrtaceae

The Myrtle or Myrtaceae family of plants is diverse and very prominent in the Gold Coast bush, and in fact, throughout Australia. They include the lilly pilly, bottlebrush, tea-tree, paperbark and the eucalypts, which includes the famous Australian gum tree. The plants come as large trees, shrubs and even some ground covers. They have a wide variety of flower forms where the flower colour often comes from its brightly coloured stamens. This is particularly noticeable in the bottlebrushes. The fruit can be hard, as in the nuts of the gum trees, or soft as in the brightly coloured berries of the lilly pillies.

Bottlebrush

9 Southport History

The oldest developed area of the Gold Coast is at Southport. The area has a rich heritage and while much has been lost to new developments there are still many areas to explore.

Southport Pier

At a glance

Grade: Easy
Time: 2 hrs 30 mins
Distance: 5.5 km return
Conditions: Some shade

Getting there

Bus: www.translink.com.au or T 13 12 30 for buses from your location

Car: Adjacent to Marine Parade (Gold Coast Highway) at Southport there is paid parking at the start of the walk near the swimming pool in the Broadwater parklands

9 Southport History

Walk directions

1 Begin at the pier adjacent to the Broadwater Parklands and swimming pool. Take a short detour onto the new pier, which replaced the original structure in 2009, where you'll see historical displays. The pier has always been part of local entertainment with swimming and fishing from its earliest days a century ago. Retrace your steps and turn left off the pier, following the concrete path with the water on your left. Along the way are signs on theatre and bathing costume history.

2 After a short distance you'll reach the swimming enclosure and Anzac Memorial. Continue following the waterside path for 800 metres. In the distance you'll see the skyscrapers of Surfers Paradise.

3 When you reach the Gold Coast Highway Bridge, retrace your steps to Nerang Street, opposite the Pier. Cross the highway at the lights into Nerang Street, the main business street of Southport. As you head up the street there are some old buildings and businesses still operating among the modern outlets.

4 Towards the end of the first block on the left-hand side is Birbeck's Jewellers established in 1912. As you come to the intersection you are at what was known as Carey's Corner and across Scarborough Street is the old Cecil Hotel. The original timber hotel built in 1908 was replaced by the current brick building in 1938. Continue following Nerang Street.

5 At the intersection with High Street, cross Nerang Street to St Peter's Anglican Church. The current church was finished in 1959, replacing the original small timber building from the 1880s. Turn right down High Street and after 100 metres you'll see, across the road, St Hilda's School; a private girls' school established by the Anglican Church in 1912.

6 Retrace your steps to the corner and cross High Street. Follow Nerang Street and veer right into Queen Street.

7 Trinity Lutheran Church is just a few paces along Queen Street. Continue along Queen Street, passing the Southport State School to Southport Cemetery. The first grave was occupied by the victim of a lightning strike in 1878. You may like to spend some time reading the inscriptions on the gravestones.

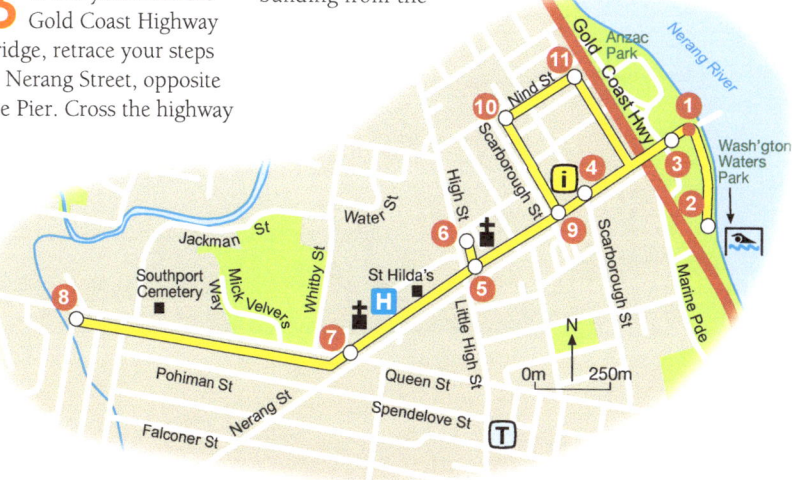

51

9 Southport History

8 Trace your steps back to the church opposite waypoint 5. Continue along Nerang Street.

9 On the corner of Davenport Street is the site of the former Queens Hotel. Cross the street to the former Town Hall, now a Gold Coast City Council office where there is an information centre with detailed heritage trail maps.
Next door, the restored ambulance station, opened in 1922, is now office space. The building on the next corner was originally the post office. Turn left into Scarborough Street.

10 At the intersection with Nind Street is the former Skeleton's Butchery. Across the road is the Railway Hotel which dates from 1889 and beyond is the Southport Transit Centre in Railway Street, the site of the former railway station which closed in 1964. Cross Scarborough Street, walking along Nind Street.

11 At the highway, turn right. In this block, Balclutha, Southport's first home, was built in 1877. Several guest houses used by holiday makers also once stood along this section of highway.
The campus of the Central Queensland University was formerly the Star of the Sea Convent. Continue on to the Nerang Street Mall, cross at the lights to the parklands and return to the pier.

Surfers Paradise

Walk variation

You can walk north through the parklands on the Broadwater Way to Labrador for about 3.5 km to reach the start of walk 10.

52

9 Southport History

Heritage Post office building

Gold Coast history – Nerang Heads

Southport was originally the land of the Yugambeh people before settlement and was first known as Nerang Heads. The first land sales were in the 1870s and the area became a holiday destination for the people of Brisbane. Early visitors came by horse-drawn vehicles or steamer until 1889 when the rail service arrived. There were many guest houses and hotels in the area and visitors enjoyed the calm waters of the Broadwater travelling by boat to explore the surf beaches. In 1925 the Jubilee Bridge opened providing access to the beaches to the south. This was later replaced by today's modern highway bridge in 1966, which led to the development we see today. As the Gold Coast developed, Southport became the service and business centre, until later years when commercial activities spread along the coast.

10 Labrador Heritage Walk

History and stories surround you on this walk along the waterfront and into the suburban streets of Labrador. Explore the environment, culture and heritage of the early days of Labrador. The walk has frequent signposts identifying heritage sites, with details on one side and local stories on the reverse side.

At a glance

Grade: Easy
Time: 2 hrs
Distance: 4.5 km circuit
Conditions: Exposed

Getting there

Bus: www.translink.com.au or T 13 12 30 for buses from your location

Car: Parking near corner of Gold Coast Highway and Marine Parade, Labrador

10 Labrador Heritage Walk

Walk directions

1 Begin at the Grand Hotel, on the corner of Marine Parade and the Gold Coast Highway in Labrador. The Grand Hotel dates from 1886 and became a popular destination for people from Brisbane. Guests were met at the Cobb and Co coach depot and later at the railway station by the hotel's elegant horse-drawn vehicle. Cross the street to follow the waterside pathway, keeping the water on your right.

2 You'll soon reach Harley Park, named after former Gold Coast Mayor Ernest Oliver Harley. Continue on to a sign about the former Labrador House which was near the intersection with Brisbane Road. This was suitably named as it was the main road to Brisbane from the Gold Coast until the development of the current highway well to the west. A little further on is Historic Marker 5 which details the history of the Labrador Hotel which opened in 1881.

3 A block further on is a group of metal fish sculptures and a signboard detailing early fishing history. Fishing was both a pastime and an occupation for the residents, with plentiful fish catches as well as oyster collecting. In winter, netting sea mullet was popular. As you walk along the waterfront, you may see paragliders and jet boats. Continue along the waterfront for one kilometre. Along the way you'll find more signs detailing the area's history.

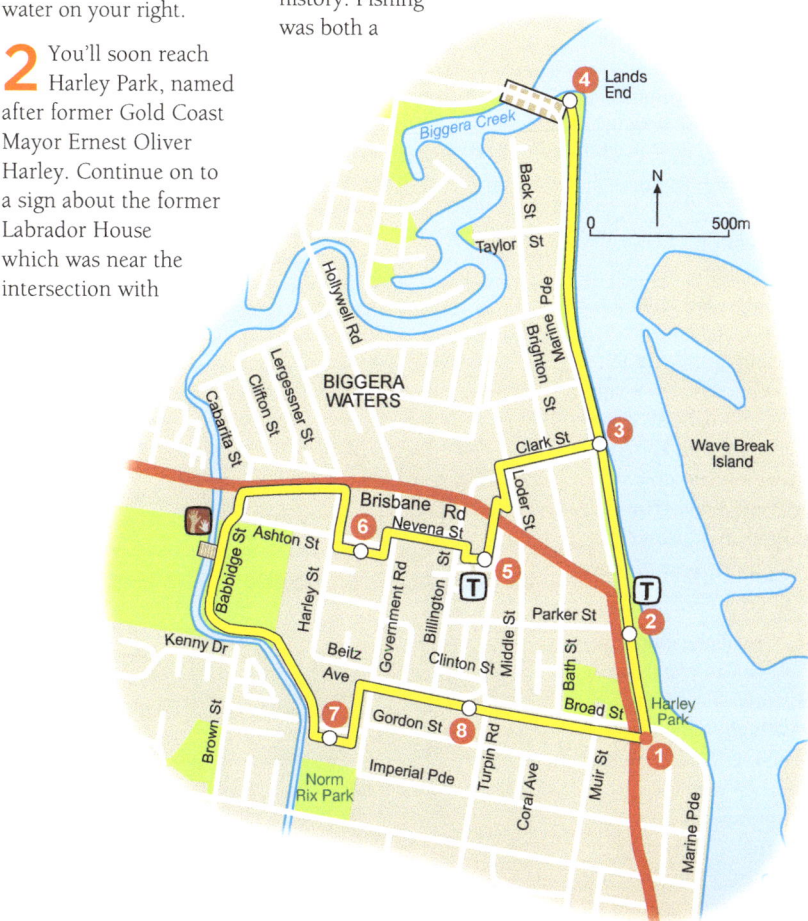

55

10 Labrador Heritage Walk

4 At Lands End where you'll meet Biggera Creek, retrace your steps back to waypoint 3. Turn right and cross Marine Parade into Clark Street. Walk for two blocks to Loder Street, then turn left and walk out to Brisbane Road. Cross Brisbane Road at the crossing and turn right. A few paces further on, at the squash centre, turn left into Turpin Road. Follow Turpin Road for 60 metres.

5 Cross the road and walk through the small park to Billington Street. A sign details the history of the original Labrador State School which opened in 1921 with 17 pupils. Some came from as far away as Stradbroke Island. Turn right to walk along Billington Street, and then left into Nevenia Street, heading uphill. Go left into Government Road, right into Ashton Street, then right into Harley Street to meet up with Brisbane Road. Turn left at Brisbane Road and head down towards the shopping centre.

6 Near the shopping centre you'll see Historic Marker 14 which gives the history of Brisbane Road. Continue on, then take the first left into Babbidge Street towards the sporting facilities. Near the bridge over the creek, you'll find Historic Marker 15 which has information about the Saltwater People, who were the original Aboriginal inhabitants of the area. Do not cross the bridge, but follow the path along this side of the creek. Skirt the oval on a concrete walkway.

7 The path eventually comes out at Norm Rix Park on Government Road opposite the site of the current Labrador State School. Historic Marker 17 provides a history of the park and details on the school. Turn left and walk uphill along Government Road. At Broad Street, cross Government Road and walk downhill.

8 At Turpin Road you'll see tall carved wooden sculptures in Tardent Park, named after Jules Louis Tardent, a Gallipoli veteran and forester. Continue along Broad Street, crossing Turpin Road and then passing two more historic markers. The walk ends at Historic Marker 21 at the Arthur Downes Memorial Hall on the corner of the main road. From here you can see The Grand Tavern, part of the Grand Hotel and the starting point of the walk.

56

10 Labrador Heritage Walk

Broadwater at Labrador

Gold Coast history – The sugar industry

The early history of the Gold Coast is steeped in rural industries. First, there were timber getters, but later a substantial sugar industry developed as early settlers were encouraged to grow sugar cane. Some of the industry remains on the northern section of the Gold Coast. At one stage there were over forty mills in the area. The remaining sugar mill at Rocky Point was established in 1879. The mill is owned by the Heck Family who came to the area in the 1860s when Carl Heck emigrated from Germany. The industry attracted settlers from a variety of countries and no doubt this is reflected in the story "From Many Places" at marker 16. It was sugar farmer Robert Muir who, with investor John Lennon, opened up the early real estate at Labrador. The mills also had distilleries – Beenleigh Distillery is still operating.

11 Coombabah Lakelands Koala Track

This is one of many tracks in the Coombabah Lakelands Conservation Area. The area is the largest mainland coastal conservation area on the Gold Coast. It is an important habitat for marine life and local and migratory birds as well as our much loved mammals, the wallaby and koala. The tracks here are signed with walking times which are one-way only.

At a glance

Grade: Easy
Time: 4 hrs
Distance: 10 km circuit
Conditions: Some shade

Getting there

Bus: Buses service nearby Coombabah High School about 1.5 km away; T 13 12 30 for timetable information

Car: Off Pine Ridge Road, Coombabah, turn into Rain Tree Glen and drive for 1 kilometre

Saltwater couch grasslands

11 Coombabah Lakelands Koala Track

Walk directions

1 The track begins on the opposite side of the road to the Southport Flying Club. Follow the Goshawk track straight ahead for about 200 metres to a sign which reads *Koala Track 35 minutes*. From here there are frequent signs. Keep a lookout for wallabies grazing nearby.

2 After about 200 metres when you reach the trees, look up – particularly at the gum trees – for koalas. After another 100 metres, veer left onto the Koala Track which cuts through the trees. The track follows the swampy edge of the lake where you'll see salt-tolerant mangrove trees. Follow this for 1.5 kilometres; do not turn off the track. Look out on your left for the sign to the Mangrove Track which you'll need for navigation on the way back.

3 The track swings to the left and you'll soon pass the entrance to the Spoonbill Track on your right. Don't take this track, but rather continue following the Koala Track. Shortly, you will come to the end of the Koala Track up against the red couch grasslands on the edge of the lake.

4 Retrace your steps for a short distance and turn left onto the Jabiru Trail. From this trail you'll get glimpses of the lake to the left with stands of tea-tree and she-oak. This can

11 Coombabah Lakelands Koala Track

be quite wet and swampy after heavy rain. The track eventually returns to the Koala Track. From here, retrace your steps looking out for the Mangrove Track turn-off which you saw earlier.

5 Opposite the Mangrove Track sign, take a short unnamed track which leads to the Robur Track. Follow the Robur Track which is eventually renamed Coucal Track. Cross the Kookaburra Track and follow the path back to waypoint 2. In a short distance you'll see the Koala Track ahead. Join the Koala Track and from here you'll be able to see the starting point.

Coombabah Lake Marshlands

11 Coombabah Lakelands Koala Track

Australian environment – Koala

The koala is a unique Australian mammal which lives mainly in eucalypt trees where it sleeps in the fork of the tree during the day. It is most active at night, particularly just after sunset when it feeds on the leaves of the tree. It rarely drinks and obtains most of its moisture from the leaves. Due to a special adaptation of its digestive system, the koala has the ability to eat the eucalypt leaves which are toxic to many animals. Baby koalas, known as joeys, live in their mother's pouch for six to seven months and then ride on her back until they become self-sufficient by 18 months of age. They are very good climbers using their sharp claws. Occasionally, you will see koalas on the ground, moving from tree to tree. When walking look high up in the eucalypt trees, particularly if there are scratch marks on the trunk close to the ground. Koalas are not easy to see but generate great excitement when found in the wild.

12 Coombabah Boardwalk

This is an easy one-way track along the edge of the creek, much of it on a well-constructed boardwalk. This makes it suitable for strollers and wheelchairs although there are a couple of unsealed parts between sections of boardwalk.

At a glance

Grade: Easy
Time: 1 hr return
Distance: 3 km return
Conditions: Some shade. Take insect repellent. No dogs.

Getting there

Bus: Gold Coast bus service route 5 Coombabah starts from Pacific Fair at Southport and stops near the corner of Georgia Street close by the start of the walk

Car: From the Gold Coast Highway at Biggera Waters follow Oxley Drive for about 4km to Hansford Road Coombabah to Citie Drive then Myola Court. Street parking adjacent to the start of the walk in, at Myola Court, Coombabah

12 Coombabah Boardwalk

Walk directions

1 Begin at the interpretive sign shelter in Myola Court, Coombabah. This is part of the very large Coombabah Lakelands Conservation Area. From here the path leads down to the edge of the creek and the start of the wooden boardwalk.

2 Just a short distance in is a small pontoon where you can relax and watch the birdlife and enjoy views along the creek. Often you will get perfect reflections in the water – great for photographers. At low tide watch for the small crabs going about their life beside and below the boardwalk, or at higher tides see if you can spot other marine life. The mangroves are important habitats for a variety of marine animals including prawns, molluscs and fish. In the branches you might see birds, snakes or lizards.

3 The boardwalk goes for about 200 metres before becoming a gravel track. Keep to the edge of the creek, ignoring all side tracks leading to nearby residences. About 350 metres further on follow another long section of boardwalk. A common tree species in this area is the swamp oak, identified by its long, thin, needle-like leaves.

4 Pass a sign with more information on the area. Follow the gravel track to an open grassy area for 200 metres to the end, at another access point and a drain. Return the way you came. Watch for wildlife and see if you can spot one of the other common trees of the area, the paperbark, so named for its soft bark which peels off in sheets. Aboriginal people used the bark when constructing shelters and for wrapping food prior to cooking.

63

12 Coombabah Boardwalk

Wattle in flower

Australian environment – Mangroves

Mangroves are a group of trees and shrubs that have adapted to live in the intertidal zone of our coastal rivers and creeks. They have a complicated root structure which allows them to withstand the pounding of the waves and changes in tidal levels. Because of the low oxygen levels in the flooded soils they have specially adapted root-like structures called pneumatophores for breathing. These are the stick-like structures you see rising out of the ground around the trees. Mangrove trees have a difficult start in life and some species overcome this by allowing their seeds to germinate on the tree. The young trees develop a sharp root structure that spears into the mud when they drop into the water. The mangroves are important in stabilising the shoreline, preventing erosion. By collecting the silt that comes down rivers they can extend the foreshore. They are also an important part of the fisheries habitat, providing a 'nursery' for young fish.

12 Coombabah Boardwalk

Coombabah Lake

Boardwalk Tallebudgera

Southern Gold Coast

The coastline of the southern Gold Coast offers the walker an amazing array of headlands, with both sheltered and exposed beaches and renowned surf breaks. The tracks pass vantage points for expansive views to the north as far as Stradbroke Island and south along the coast to Fingal Head and Cape Byron, Australia's most easterly point. To the west are the hinterland and the valleys of the rivers and creeks. The lookouts and beaches also offer places to watch boardriders, migrating whales and playful dolphins. Reaching the coast are rivers and creeks which flow from the lush hinterland. These waterways offer spots to fish or swim. History abounds, with memorials and stories of shipwrecks, wars and remarkable citizens who have both contributed to the development of the coast and devoted their lives to the service of others. These tracks along the coast offer the opportunity for a post-walk picnic in the many parks and in summer a cooling ocean swim, but be sure to swim only between the lifesavers' flags.

Kirra Beach

13 Point Danger to Coolangatta

In May 1770, Captain James Cook, while sailing north along the coast, noted the presence of shoals in his log book and wrote: "The point off which these shoals lay I have named Point Danger". Beginning at Point Danger on the Queensland–New South Wales border, this walk follows the coast north to Coolangatta Beach, before turning inland to explore Coolangatta's shopping and business precinct and returning along the State border back to Point Danger. Coolangatta was named after the schooner wrecked off the beach in 1846.

At a glance

Grade: Easy
Time: 2 hrs
Distance: 3.5 km return
Conditions: Mostly exposed

Getting there:

Bus: Bus service to Coolangatta town centre, then walk 1 kilometre to Point Danger

Car: From Griffith Street, the main business street of Coolangatta, go straight ahead along Boundary Street to Point Danger. There is parking at the corner of Boundary Street and Tweed Terrace

Tweed River

13 Point Danger to Coolangatta

Walk directions

1 Begin at the Captain Cook monument near the corner of Boundary Street and Tweed Terrace at Point Danger. Here you'll find a wealth of information and monuments to explore as well as views along the coast. Pick up the concrete path, keeping the ocean on your right. After 100 metres you'll find the Centaur Remembrance Walk, as well as other memorials to those who have served and died for their country. The adjacent information board explains the sand bypass system which moves sand from south of the Tweed River onto the beaches to the north. Follow the concrete walkway which has embedded plaques.

2 Near the intersection of Petrie Terrace and Marine Parade, turn downhill. The track turns right onto a zigzag boardwalk to the beach below. On the cliff face is a rock painted to resemble a green frog. Follow the path round Snapper Rocks and Lifeguard Tower 1 and onto sheltered and patrolled Rainbow Beach. Pass the Surf Club, which was formed in 1963. Stroll along the level path taking in the views, not forgetting the buildings on the left-hand side. The apartment buildings include St George Holiday House for serving and ex-servicemen. At the far end of the beach is Greenmount Hill.

3 Leave the beach and follow the track around the base of Greenmount Hill. Keep an eye out for wildlife such as bush turkeys and other birds and lizards. On the way you may like to make a short detour to Billy Rack Lookout, up some 20 steps. Forty metres further on is another detour of 90 stairs to the top of Greenmount Hill which has good views along the coast. Retrace your steps back to the coastal track.

4 As you come round the hill look out for a plaque and, above you, the restored Shark Sighting Tower, built in the 1960s. The hill was

69

13 Point Danger to Coolangatta

Point Danger

the site of the former Greenmount Guesthouse which opened in 1905 and was demolished in 1978. The beach ahead of you is Greenmount. Walk along the sand or follow the concrete path. Pass Lifeguard Tower 2 and head along the Coolangatta beachfront. There are many places offering refreshments on the opposite side of the road. As you approach Warner Street there is a Returned Servicemen's League memorial to the 508 men and women from the Twin Towns area who served in World War II. The clock in this memorial celebrates the golden jubilee of Rotary in 1955. At this spot is a directory board to other local spots and a cairn outlining the history of Coolangatta from 1840 to 1974.

5 Just past the Coolangatta Surf Life Saving Club and Lifeguard Tower 3 is a memorial to those who served in World War I. Turn left to the traffic lights on McLean Street and cross Marine Parade. Use the traffic lights to cross to adjacent Kirra Hill for more views and to get a close look at the Sea Eagle sculpture and the site of the first Coolangatta School. Again there is a plaque pointing out the more distant features. Return to McLean Street, walking away from the beach. Take the first left into Griffith Street, the main business and shopping street of Coolangatta. Walk for 800 metres along the left side of Griffith Street.

6 Near the intersection of Clarke Street, in the centre of the road, you'll see a monument to surveyor Francis Edward Roberts who, from 1863 to 1866, surveyed the border between the two states. At this point, Griffith Street turns right and crosses into New South Wales. Just ahead on the right is Twin Towns Services Resort and Club. Continue straight ahead along Boundary Street which takes you back, after 800 metres, to Point Danger and waypoint 1.

Walk variation

From Kirra Hill you can join Walk 18 to Currumbin along the Oceanway Walk or as you walk along Griffith Street, at the intersection with Warner Street, turn right and join Walk 15 to Razorback.

13 Point Danger to Coolangatta

Path to Duronbah

Australian history – Gold Coast and war

The Gold Coast has had a long association with the military. In 1828, a military post was established at Point Danger to recapture escaped convicts from the Moreton Bay settlement. Later, local residents were involved in all of the major conflicts and they are remembered by memorials and plaques along the coast; particularly along the waterfront, but also in parks across the coast.

With fears of invasion during World War II, US troops arrived on the Gold Coast in 1942 and in 1945 a US Military Base was established at Point Danger. Later the coast became a favoured holiday and retirement place for war veterans.

Today on Point Danger there are several memorials including one to the Australian hospital ship *Centaur* which was torpedoed by the Japanese off the southern Queensland coast in May 1943 with the loss of 268 lives. There were 64 survivors who waited 36 hours before being rescued. The exact whereabouts of the ship remained a mystery until it was located in December 2009.

14 Point Danger to the Tweed River

You'll be able to say you walked between two states on this track. The walk starts at Point Danger on the Queensland–New South Wales border and covers the famous Duranbah Beach and the entrance to the Tweed River. There are views to the south to Fingal Head lighthouse and west to the mountains.

North from Point Danger

At a glance

Grade: Easy
Time: 1 hr
Distance: 3 km return
Conditions: Mostly exposed

Getting there:

Bus: Bus service to Coolangatta town centre, then walk 1 kilometre to Point Danger

Car: From Griffith Street, the main business street of Coolangatta, go straight ahead along Boundary Street to Point Danger. There is parking at the corner of Boundary Street and Tweed Terrace

14 Point Danger to the Tweed River

Walk directions

1 Begin at the Captain Cook monument at Point Danger near the corner of Boundary Street and Tweed Terrace. To the south is the Tweed River and beyond, Fingal Head. To the north are views along the Gold Coast. Below is the famous Duranbah Beach with excellent views of the surfboard riders in action. Take the footpath to the south of the monument, keeping the ocean on your left. You have now crossed into New South Wales. Cross the road to Carlin Park where there is a memorial to the Rats of Tobruk and a sign which tells the story of the Mediterranean Fleet's involvement in the siege of Tobruk. Return to the footpath across the road and take the steep path and steps leading downhill for 150 metres.

2 At the end of the path turn left onto the road to explore the area under the Point Danger cliffs. One hundred metres past the end of the road you will find the first of the outflow pipes from the Tweed Sand Bypass. The rocky basalt cliffs are characteristic of the remnants of ancient volcanic activity which formed many of the rocky headlands on the Gold Coast and on the beaches of northern New South Wales. Retrace your steps to waypoint 2 and then pick up the path which follows Duranbah Beach, a famous surfing beach, sometimes referred to as D'bah (pronounced "Dee-bah").

3 After 200 metres you'll reach the northern sea wall at the mouth of the Tweed River. If the weather and sea conditions are calm, it's possible to walk to the end of the sea wall. Take note of the various warning signs. The sea wall has a wide gravel track and is about 350 metres long. Along the seawall are good vantage points to watch the surfboard

73

14 Point Danger to the Tweed River

Duranbah and Tweed River from Point Danger

riders with the backdrop of Point Danger and the coast to the north. Duranbah was named after the coastal steamer which foundered here in 1919 and was later the site of the first Billabong Pro surfing competition in 1984. Follow the concrete pathway along the Tweed River bank. The river was named and discovered by John Oxley in 1823.

4 Pick up the concrete walkway which skirts John Follent park. Continue on past the memorial to the *Ebenezer* which was wrecked in 1859. After another 50 metres on the riverside path, you'll reach the Jack Evans Boat Harbour. Jack ran the Snapper Rocks Pool in the early tourist days of the southern Gold Coast. He had a swimming pool and shark pool in the mid 1950s and later, a dolphin show. The venue moved to Duranbah in 1961. Follow Coral Street which curves away from the water.

5 When Coral Street meets Boundary Street, cross Boundary Street and turn right. To the left are the Twin Towns Resort and Club. Walk uphill along Boundary Street for 450 metres to Point Danger and your starting point.

Start of Oceanway at Point Danger

Walk variation

From waypoint 4 follow the waterside path around the Jack Evans Boat Harbour, past the Tweed Heads War Memorial, to the shopping centre of Tweed Heads.

14 Point Danger to the Tweed River

Water safety – Volunteer Marine Rescue Centres

The Gold Coast is a mecca for boating with wonderful access to the Pacific Ocean, the Southport Broadwater and the waters of Southern Moreton Bay. However, at times there are difficult bars to cross, and waters and weather to be negotiated. There are three Volunteer Marine Rescue Association centres on the Gold Coast. They are located at the Southport Seaway, at the mouth of Currumbin Creek and at the mouth of the Tweed River.

The centres are staffed by volunteers who provide advice, information, radio monitoring and a reporting network and rescue service to the boating community. The Point Danger unit was formed in 1965 and soon after followed by Southport. They were among the first established in Queensland.

The Volunteer Marine Rescue Association by agreement with the Queensland Government is the responsible body for Volunteer Marine Rescue Services in Queensland, with twenty-five centres reaching from Point Danger to Thursday Island and the Gulf of Carpentaria, and a fleet of rescue boats and radio networks.

15 Razorback

From central Coolangatta this more strenuous walk goes through a local park then takes in Razorback Lookout and ends at the Tom Beatson Lookout. From here are views to the north and east over the twin towns of Tweed Heads and Coolangatta. Further south is Fingal Head and Cook Island. On the other side to the west are views over the Tweed Valley, Gold Coast International Airport and the mountain peaks and ranges of northern New South Wales, Mt Warning and the Gold Coast hinterland, including Springbrook.

At a glance

Grade: Medium
Time: 2 hrs
Distance: 4 km return
Conditions: Mostly exposed

Getting there:

Bus: www.translink.com.au or T 13 12 30 for services from your area

Car: Take Marine Parade at Coolangatta along the beachfront where there is parking on the beachfront and in streets behind the shopping precinct

View to Coolangatta and Tweed Heads

15 Razorback

Walk directions

1 Begin at the beachfront at the intersection of Warner Street and Marine Parade. Here you will find several signs and monuments of interest including a plaque on the history of the area from 1870 to 1974. Walk along Warner Street away from the beach, crossing Griffith Street, the main shopping precinct of Coolangatta. Continue on to Lanham Street and you will find the Coolangatta Transit Centre on the right and the Bowls Club on the left. In front of you is the intersection of Scott and Lanham Streets where you cross into Goodwin Park. About 200 metres into the park is a war memorial and just beyond, to the left-hand side, is Carmichael Close.

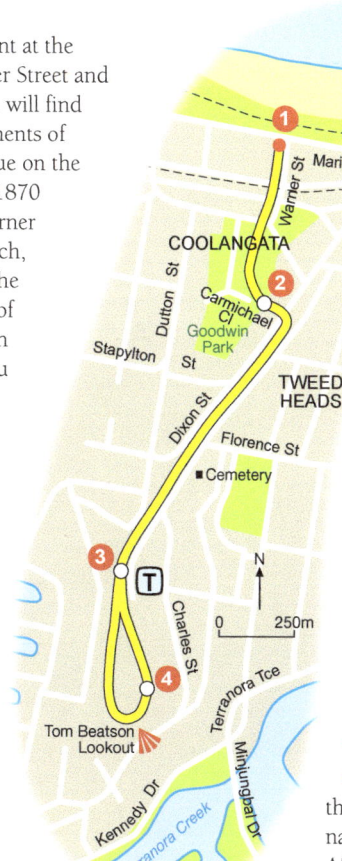

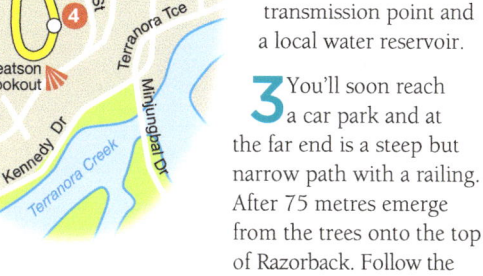

2 Walk up Carmichael Close. This is where the level track finishes and it is all uphill from here. At the end of Carmichael Close turn right into Dixon Street. Here you will notice another road running parallel. You are now walking along the Queensland–New South Wales border. Five hundred metres up Dixon Street is a roundabout. Cross here into Charles Street and walk past a cemetery on the left-hand side. A quarter of a kilometre further on, where the road forks, turn into Razorback Road on the right-hand side. Follow the road for 300 metres, passing a Broadcast Australia transmission point and a local water reservoir.

3 You'll soon reach a car park and at the far end is a steep but narrow path with a railing. After 75 metres emerge from the trees onto the top of Razorback. Follow the sealed circuit path, mown lawns and well-tended gardens.

4 At the top is the Tom Beatson Lookout. The views encompass the Tweed Heads district for which John Boyd selected the land in 1869. On the southern side of the river is the Fingal Lighthouse established in 1872. Return the same way and enjoy the downhill walk back to the beachfront.

77

15 Razorback

Goodwin Park

Walk variation

You could add this to either Walk 13 or 14 to make it a bit more challenging or deviate into the Tweed Heads area.

15 Razorback

Tweed River

Gold Coast environment – Protecting the beaches

The white sands of the Gold Coast beaches have formed over long periods of geological time. Under the influence of the tides, currents, wind and weather, the sands are forever moving in a northerly direction. Evidence of this is that the mouth of the Nerang River was opposite Nerang Street in Southport in 1895.

In many places the frontal dunes have been developed for housing, however, at Palm Beach and the Spit you can still see the frontal dunes. A major beach restoration project at Kirra will reform some of the dunes. At many spots along the coast the remaining dunes have been fenced off and revegetated with native and salt-tolerant species to minimise the impact of rough seas.

In other areas, in order to protect properties it has been necessary to build rock retaining walls. Rock groynes, reaching out into the ocean, protect the mouths of creeks and rivers by reducing silting and ensuring safe passage for boats. Sand bypasses are in operation at both the Tweed River and Southport Seaway.

After rough seas the beach can become steeper as sand is washed away and cliffs form on the beach. Eventually the action of the waves will restore the gentle slope of the beach.

16 Kirra to Currumbin

Beginning with an easy beachside stroll you'll see Kirra's famous surf break which has been described by surfers as "totally epic". You'll stroll by examples of modern beachside mansions which provide a contrast to the remaining, more modest fibro shacks of times gone by.

Flat Rock

At a glance

Grade: Easy
Time: 3 hrs
Distance: 7 km one way
Conditions: Exposed

Getting there

Bus: www.translink.com.au or T 13 12 30 for services from your area. At the end of the walk, there is a stop for the bus service back to Kirra Beach on Teemangum Street and Kropp Lane

Car: Parking on the Kirra beachfront near corner of Marine Parade and Miles Street, Coolangatta

16 Kirra to Currumbin

Fibro beach shack

Walk directions

1 Start at Kirra Surf Life Saving Club, off Marine Parade, adjacent to Lifeguard Tower 4. The Club, established in 1916, hosted the first local Surf Life Saving Championships in 1928. With the ocean on your left, walk 150 metres along the pathway, south to a refurbished shelter shed. The Kirra surf break is a famous spot with surfboard riders. Just above on Kirra Hill is a sculpture of a sea eagle by artist Craig Medson. Retrace your steps back to the Life Saving Club and now with the ocean on your right, follow the sealed path along the beachfront. You'll pass she-oaks, pandanus palms and Norfolk Island pines.

Silver Gull

Gold Coast history – Coolangatta School

On top of Kirra Hill, close to the entrance to the lookout parking area, is the site of the first Coolangatta State School. It was built in 1920 as a two room school and opened with 67 students and two teachers. It was later modified many times, including in 1923, 1934, the 1950s and 1970s, before the site became too small and it moved to its current location in the 1970s.

The school also operated as a Special School and continued in this role until 2006 when the site was closed and a new facility opened in the Currumbin Valley.

It is now being restored as a part of the southern Gold Coast's heritage and a Conservation Management Plan was developed in 2007.

16 Kirra to Currumbin

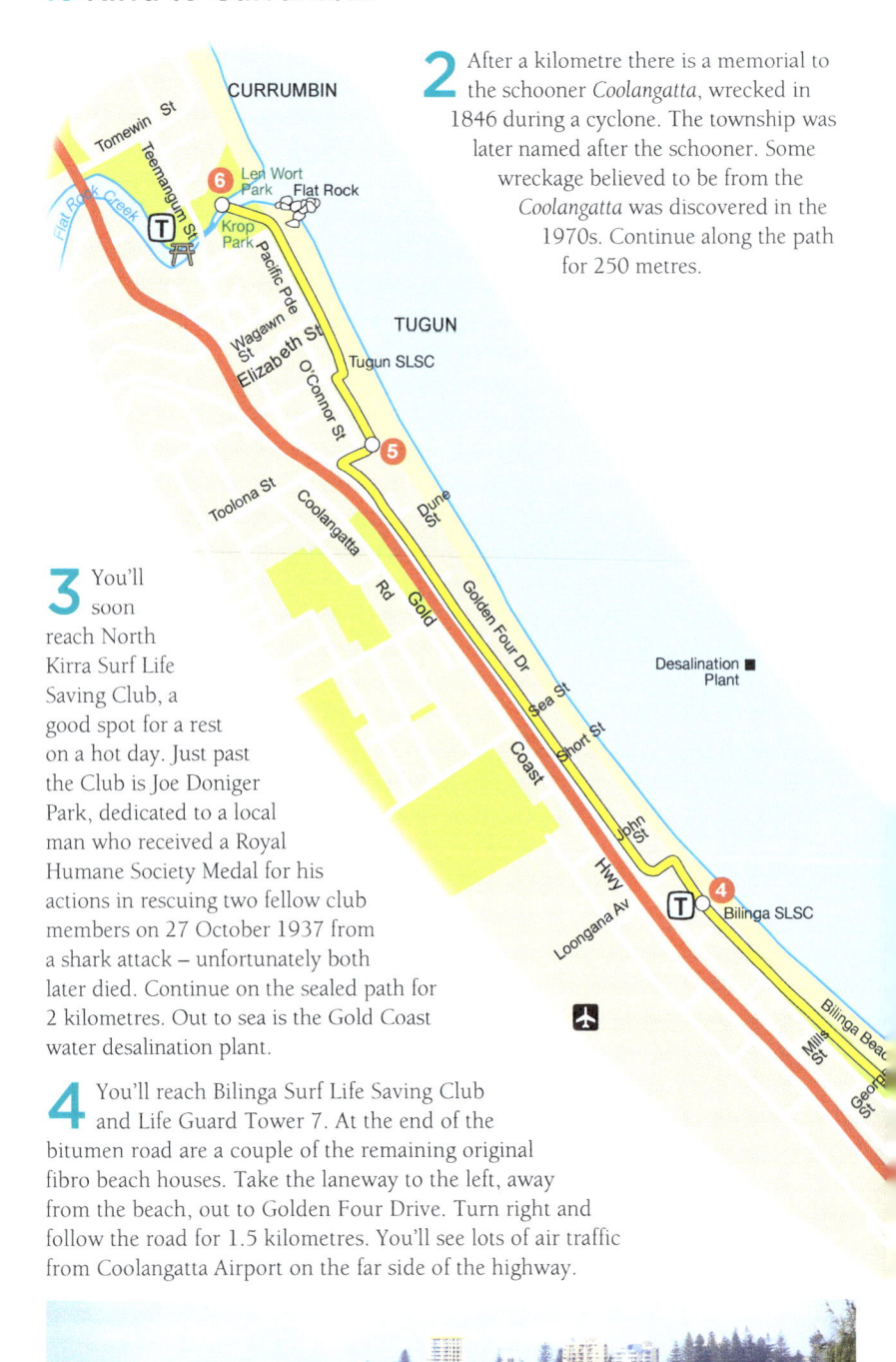

2 After a kilometre there is a memorial to the schooner *Coolangatta*, wrecked in 1846 during a cyclone. The township was later named after the schooner. Some wreckage believed to be from the *Coolangatta* was discovered in the 1970s. Continue along the path for 250 metres.

3 You'll soon reach North Kirra Surf Life Saving Club, a good spot for a rest on a hot day. Just past the Club is Joe Doniger Park, dedicated to a local man who received a Royal Humane Society Medal for his actions in rescuing two fellow club members on 27 October 1937 from a shark attack – unfortunately both later died. Continue on the sealed path for 2 kilometres. Out to sea is the Gold Coast water desalination plant.

4 You'll reach Bilinga Surf Life Saving Club and Life Guard Tower 7. At the end of the bitumen road are a couple of the remaining original fibro beach houses. Take the laneway to the left, away from the beach, out to Golden Four Drive. Turn right and follow the road for 1.5 kilometres. You'll see lots of air traffic from Coolangatta Airport on the far side of the highway.

Greenmount and Rainbow Bay

16 Kirra to Currumbin

5 At the Tugun Tavern on Toolona Street turn right and rejoin the beachfront path. Walk past the Tugun Surf Life Saving Club. Half a kilometre on is Flat Rock to your right and, a little further on, Kropp Park. The Kropp family has made a significant contribution to the area and Marshall Kropp was manager of the Gold Coast Lifeguard Service for fourteen seasons. A plaque provides the details. Follow the path through the park.

6 The wooden footbridge over Flat Rock Creek is the finish point of this walk. Nearby on the corner of Teemangum Street and Kropp Lane is a stop for the bus service back to Kirra Beach.

Coolangatta Shipwreck Memorial

Kropp Park bridge

83

17 Currumbin

Explore the Currumbin beachfront and then continue alongside the Currumbin Estuary and the southern bank of Currumbin Creek, a popular picnic and fishing spot. The walk passes the well-known local geological features of Elephant Rock and Currumbin Rock and a number of art features and memorials.

Elephant Rock

At a glance
Grade: Easy
Time: 2 hrs
Distance: 6 km return
Conditions: Mostly exposed

Getting there:
Bus: Stops near Len Wort Park, close to the Currumbin Bird Sanctuary; www.translink.com.au or T 13 12 30 for services from your area

Car: Parking near Len Wort Park, Teenamgum Street, Currumbin

17 Currumbin

Walk directions

1 Begin at Len Wort Park off Teenamgum Street, Currumbin, where there are good playground and picnic facilities. Pick up the oceanside track which leads off to the left towards the beach, keeping the water on your right. Pass in front of the beachfront residences and, after about 200 metres, join a footpath at the corner of Pacific Parade and Tomewin Street. Follow the path along the beachfront.

2 A further 500 metres brings you to Elephant Rock. It's worth the side trip to the lookout on the top of the rock. There are 65 steps to negotiate, but excellent views along the coast. The first 19 steps lead to the entrance of the 90-year-old Currumbin Surf Life Saving Club and a further 46 narrow concrete steps take you to the top. After taking in the views, return to the footpath along the roadway. Over to your left are changing rooms, shops and cafés, while on the beachfront is a patrolled surfing area. Follow the beachfront for 600 metres.

3 Opposite the Rocks Resort is a wooden platform with a bronze statue of a bikini-clad sunbather, depicting a lifestyle which has made the coast famous.

4 A little further on, you'll reach the mouth of Currumbin Creek and Currumbin Alley, a very popular surfboard riding spot, but only for very experienced riders. The breakwater leads out to Currumbin Rock. There are many good viewing areas for watching the surfers. If you'd like to learn to surf, there are classes available in the area. Continue along the waterside path as it follows the creek inland. Be sure to read the plaque at the road end of the spit which explains the area's role as a National Environmental Sanctuary dedicated to the study of geology and marine biology. Continue along the path into Duringan Street.

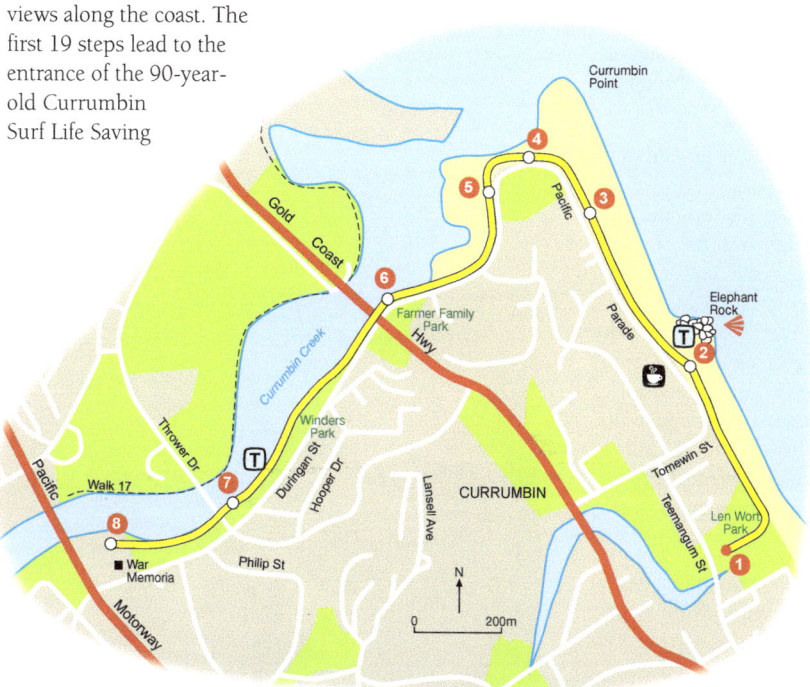

85

17 Currumbin

5 You'll soon reach the Volunteer Marine Rescue Station, one of many located along the coast. About five hundred metres on is Farmer Family Park. This was named in recognition of the family's significant contribution to the Surf Life Saving movement on the Gold Coast. Here there is a statue to celebrate the life of Beryl Carnell, a pioneer of tourism and entertainment on the Gold Coast.

6 Pass under the Gold Coast Highway bridge and walk on to Winders Park. This is a well-equipped park for BBQs and picnics and is also a good spot for fishing in Currumbin Creek. On the creek bank is a collection of eleven metal sculptures of pelicans in a range of typical poses. Follow the path for 700 metres.

7 At the far end of the park is Throwers Bridge, the original road bridge over the creek. Cross the road at the pedestrian lights at the bridge and continue along the creek past the tennis centre, over the small pedestrian bridge to the Currumbin RSL Club with its memorial to our servicemen and women from many theatres of war.

8 From the memorial, retrace your steps back to the starting point.

Currumbin RSL Memorial

View north from Elephant Rock

17 Currumbin

Walk variation

Walk over Throwers Bridge at waypoint 7 and join the Palm Beach walk (Walk 18).

Currumbin Beach and Alley

Out and about – Swell Sculpture Festival

If you are lucky enough to be at Currumbin in September, check the dates for the Swell Sculpture Festival. This is an outdoor visual arts exhibition of some 50 sculptures which runs for ten days in September on the beachfront between the mouth of Currumbin Creek and Elephant Rock along the beachfront. There is a wonderful and creative range of sculptures using a diverse array of materials. As well as viewing the art, you can take part in a range of activities including workshops, talks and walks. If you cannot be there for Swell, there are examples of the works which are now fixtures on the coast and you will pass them on this walk. On the beachfront is the beach girl and further around on the banks of Currumbin Creek are the pelican sculptures. The Swell Festival is now an established and popular event on the southern Gold Coast.

18 Palm Beach

On the northern side of Currumbin Creek there are wetlands and beaches to explore, and you'll have fine views of Currumbin and the hinterland mountains. The well-formed track has large sections of boardwalk and if you're an angler, don't forget your fishing gear. With a large pirate-themed playground and cafés close to the turnaround point, this can be a good family walk.

At a glance

Grade: Easy
Time: 1 hr 30 mins
Distance: 4 km return
Conditions: Mostly exposed

Getting there:

Bus: www.translink.com.au or T 13 12 30 for services from your area

Car: Parking off Thrower Drive, Palm Beach on ocean side of bridge, adjacent to Palm Beach Swimming Pool

Dogs: Permitted on some parts of the track

18 Palm Beach

Walk directions

1 Begin in the car park near Throwers Bridge on Thrower Drive, Palm Beach. In the left-hand corner of the car park find the sign indicating Beree Badalla Reserve and the start of the boardwalk track. This is a wide, well-surfaced track suitable for strollers and bikes. The reserve is part of a declared fish habitat providing breeding grounds for fish such as bream and flathead as well as banana prawns. You'll pass salt-tolerant trees including she-oaks which have narrow, needle-like leaves, and grey and yellow mangroves which have large, rounded leaves. The short grass is marine couch and the succulent-like plants are samphires.

2 After about 500 metres pass under the Gold Coast Highway

89

18 Palm Beach

Bridge. Stay with the main path along the creek ignoring side exits to the left. From here there are views across the estuary to Currumbin Rock. There are popular fishing spots along this bank and places to rest and take in the views and the birdlife. The track is sealed and winds around the next bay known as Currumbin Lagoon, through pandanus palms and banksia trees in the Tarrabora Reserve.

3 Emerge from the trees to meet a pirate-themed playground. There is a café at the opposite end of the reserve. The playground has a large pirate ship with all manner of pirate-themed activities, including walking the plank. Continue on the concrete path, passing residential buildings on the left and an area of dune restoration on the right. There is also a large dog off-leash area.

4 About 200 metres past the pirate playground, leave the sealed path and follow the sandy track ahead, heading towards Lifeguard Tower 13 and a patrolled beach.

5 Turn right onto the beach and walk for 500 metres towards the mouth of Currumbin Creek.

6 You'll reach a rock wall at the end of the beach. There is no walking path along the rock wall which is rough and can be slippery. At the end of the wall is a navigation tower which is a favourite spot for ocean birds to nest. About 150 metres back along the beach, find a sandy path which cuts through the trees of the dune restoration area. This leads back to the parkland reserve. From here retrace your steps back to waypoint 1.

Water safety – Lifesavers and lifeguards

Always swim between the red and yellow flags to enjoy the Gold Coast's rolling surf. The patrols between the flags are provided by the Surf Lifesaving Association and the Gold Coast Lifeguard Service.

The Surf Life Saving movement is run by volunteers on weekends and holiday periods during the surfing season. The network of clubs along the coast has a rich history and a proud record of achievement since the movement began at Sydney's Manly Beach in 1902. The red and yellow patrol flags were introduced in Queensland in 1935 with the first reel and line rescue at Greenmount Beach in 1909. Today the service has a range of fast rescue boats and jetskis supported by helicopter patrols as well as the more traditional techniques to deliver rescue, first aid and patrol services. Many of the clubs have restaurants and entertainment which provide financial support. The lifesaving movement has achieved worldwide recognition for their dedication, service and courage.

At other times, members of the Gold Coast City Council Lifeguard Service patrol the beaches. They are Australia's largest professional lifeguard service, and cover 26 beaches all year and 42 during the holiday season. You can spot their distinctive yellow patrol towers along the beachfront.

18 Palm Beach

Walk variation

For a much longer walk you can link this track and the Currumbin walk (Walk 17) together. As you return to the start just before the Gold Coast Highway bridge, find a path to the right which will take you up to a path over the bridge.

19 Palm Beach to Tallebudgera

Explore the beaches and streets on the surf side of the Gold Coast Highway on this walk, where you'll see a mix of old and new beachside architecture. If it gets a bit too warm for walking, there are patrolled beaches for a cooling swim in the surf or the quieter waters of Tallebudgera Creek. There's the opportunity to learn about local Indigenous groups and spots for watching board riders enjoying the surf breaks.

At a glance

Grade: Easy
Time: 2 hrs
Distance: 5 km one way
Conditions: Exposed

Getting there

Bus: www.translink.com.au or T 13 12 30 for services from your area

Car: Park at Palm Beach Parklands, corner Gold Coast Highway and Thrower Drive, Palm Beach. For a car shuffle, park the other car near the Tallebudgera Creek Bridge.

Palm Beach

19 Palm Beach to Tallebudgera

Walk directions

1 Start at the parking and playground area at Palm Beach Parklands near the corner of the Gold Coast Highway and Thrower Drive, Palm Beach. Pick up the main sealed pathway which veers left and heads towards the beach. This is the Rockview Public Parkway. Keeping the ocean on your right, continue on for 300 metres past the car park. The pathway will turn left, away from the beach.

2 Turn right into Jefferson Lane, a narrow one-way street through the beachfront houses of Palm Beach. Modern beach houses have replaced most of the older architecture. After 800 metres you'll pass, on your right, the Palm Beach Surf Life Saving Club, established in 1930. Continue on for 1 kilometre. Along the way you'll see rock walls similar to those built at the entrances of many coastal creeks and rivers. These have been built to trap the sand flowing north. This is part of a beach restoration method to protect beachfront properties and replace the sand lost during cyclonic seas.

Tallebudgera Lifeguard Tower

Indigenous display on pathway

19 Palm Beach to Tallebudgera

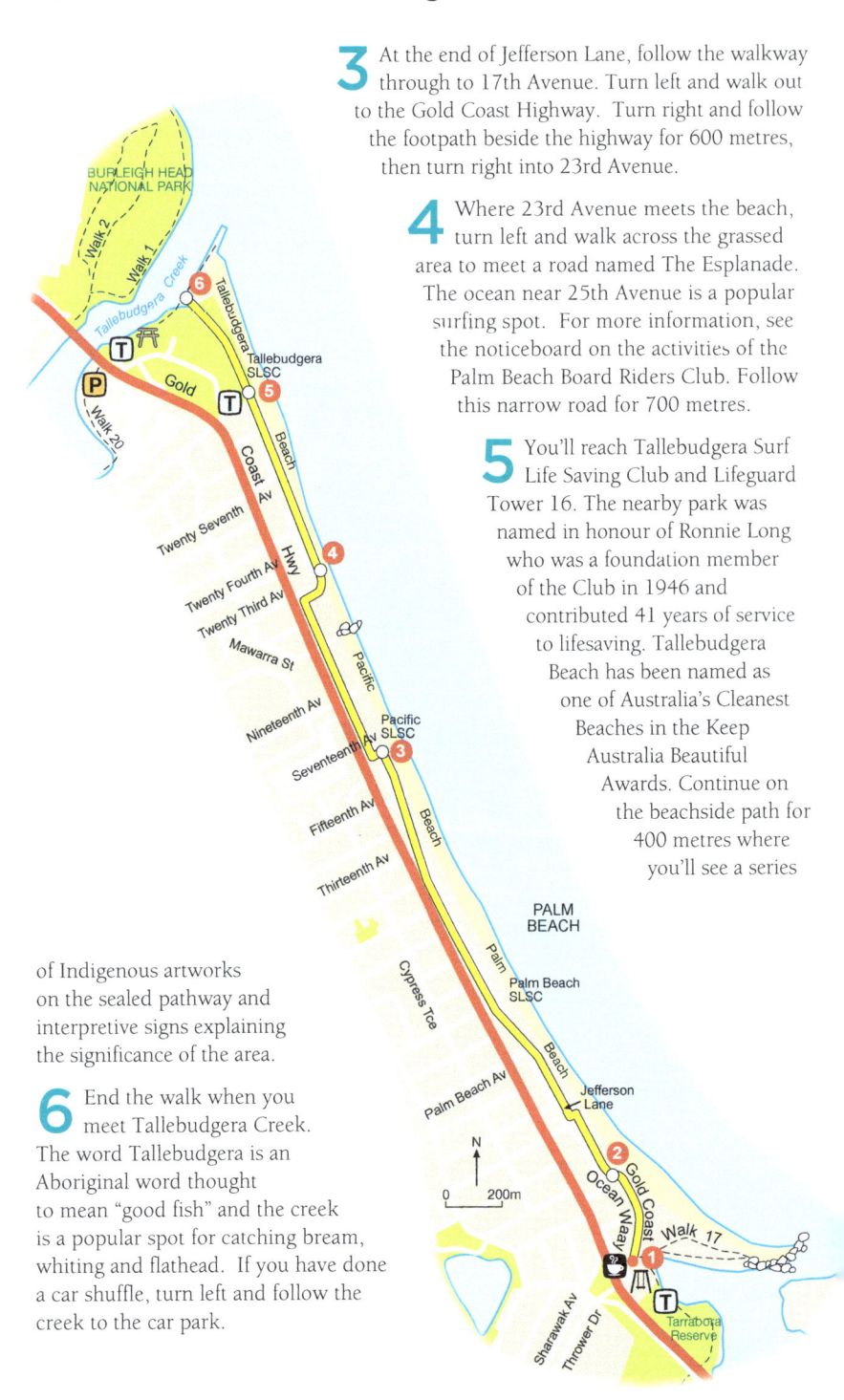

3 At the end of Jefferson Lane, follow the walkway through to 17th Avenue. Turn left and walk out to the Gold Coast Highway. Turn right and follow the footpath beside the highway for 600 metres, then turn right into 23rd Avenue.

4 Where 23rd Avenue meets the beach, turn left and walk across the grassed area to meet a road named The Esplanade. The ocean near 25th Avenue is a popular surfing spot. For more information, see the noticeboard on the activities of the Palm Beach Board Riders Club. Follow this narrow road for 700 metres.

5 You'll reach Tallebudgera Surf Life Saving Club and Lifeguard Tower 16. The nearby park was named in honour of Ronnie Long who was a foundation member of the Club in 1946 and contributed 41 years of service to lifesaving. Tallebudgera Beach has been named as one of Australia's Cleanest Beaches in the Keep Australia Beautiful Awards. Continue on the beachside path for 400 metres where you'll see a series of Indigenous artworks on the sealed pathway and interpretive signs explaining the significance of the area.

6 End the walk when you meet Tallebudgera Creek. The word Tallebudgera is an Aboriginal word thought to mean "good fish" and the creek is a popular spot for catching bream, whiting and flathead. If you have done a car shuffle, turn left and follow the creek to the car park.

19 Palm Beach to Tallebudgera

Gold Coast environment – Tugun Desalination Plant

Just off the coast at Tugun you can see the structure that is part of the Tugun Desalination Plant. This is a reverse osmosis desalination plant providing water to the South-East Queensland Water Grid. The grid was established in 2007 and is designed to link various water supplies in South-East Queensland to ensure water for residents and businesses. From about 2005 to 2009 South-East Queensland experienced its worst drought in one hundred years and there were fears that the region would run out of water. This was despite residents and businesses drastically cutting their consumption from an average of 300 litres per person per day to 115 litres. The plant has potential to produce 125 megalitres a day but production can be scaled back to meet the demand. It has not been required since the drought broke and has been mothballed.

20 Tallebudgera Creek

An easy track along the southern side of Tallebudgera Creek, the majority of the walk is along a sealed pathway. There are plenty of good views across the creek to Burleigh Headland and from the end of the breakwater along the beaches to the south. There are also plenty of picnic spots as well as swimming areas.

Tallebudgera Creek

At a glance

Grade: Easy
Time: 1 hr 30 min
Distance: 3.5 km return
Conditions: Mostly exposed

Getting there

Bus: www.translink.com.au or T 13 12 30 for services from your area

Car: Follow the Gold Coast Highway to Tallebudgera Creek. Parking on the ocean side just south of the Tallebudgera Creek bridge

20 Tallebudgera Creek

Walk directions

1 Begin at the car park just south of the Tallebudgera Creek bridge, and head for the creek bank where you will find a sealed walkway. Turn right towards the ocean. Pass the Neptune Royal Surf Life Saving Club whose members patrol the creek swimming area marked by the red and yellow flags. Proceed along the path past some shaded resting or picnic spots. To your right is the Queensland Government Sports and Leisure Centre.

2 At a fork in the track, take the left turn which leads to Tallebubgera Creek entrance, passing through a 100-metre avenue of coastal she-oaks which have long, thin, needle-like leaves. Just beyond here, the sealed path is replaced by a well-made gravel track. As you walk out to the man-made breakwater, there are views across the creek to Burleigh Headland National Park. In the other direction are views along the straight beaches to Currumbin and Point Danger. The Breakwater is a popular fishing spot and a good place to watch the boats negotiating their way out to sea or returning.

Silver Gull

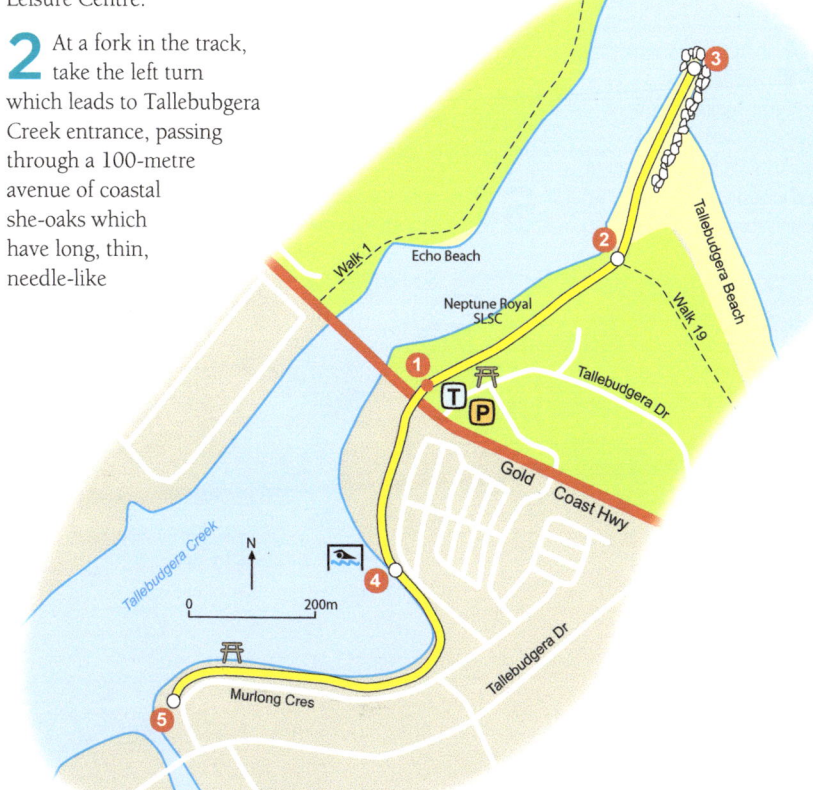

20 Tallebudgera Creek

Tallebudgera bridge

3 Retrace your steps towards the car park and walk under the road bridge.

4 After 250 metres you'll reach a swimming enclosure popular with holiday makers from the adjacent Tallebudgera Creek Tourist Park. Past the swimming area, the track crosses onto a grassy bank along the road, providing picnic areas complete with BBQ and boating facilities. Continue following the creek for another 500 metres passing a boat ramp and playgrounds.

5 The creek's beach comes to an end at a private home. This is one of the Gold Coast's largest creeks. It rises in the Springbrook Plateau where there are a variety of rainforest walks (see Walks 28 to 33). Turn around and retrace your steps back to waypoint 1 and the car park.

20 Tallebudgera Creek

Casuarina or she-oak trees

Gold Coast history – A place in the history of rock and roll

The area now occupied by the car park was once the site of the Playroom. This was one of the top live music venues in Australia and famous for its rock and roll concerts from the mid-sixties until its demolition in 1999. In its heyday from the sixties to the eighties, it hosted many famous bands and stars including Johnny O'Keefe, Australian Crawl and Cold Chisel. The licensee was Beryl Carnell who was Queensland's first female nightclub licensee, and is remembered with a statue in Farmer Park on the side of Currumbin Creek close to the site of the original Playroom.

Cameron Falls

Hinterland North – Tamborine

Tamborine Mountain is a jewel in Queensland's Scenic Rim, an arc of mountains which stretches south to the Queensland–New South Wales border, along the Border Ranges and west to the Great Dividing Range. The elevation and higher rainfall of the area offers a cooler environment than along the coast. Just over half an hour's drive from the Gold Coast, this hinterland area was formed by volcanic activity and is a wonderland of rainforest walks, waterfalls and lush gardens. It's no surprise that the area is popular with tourists who are well catered for with restaurants, coffee shops, art galleries and craft and antique shops. Those walkers who are foodies will find wineries, boutique food stores, a cheese factory and roadside stalls with locally grown produce. While none of the national parks has camping facilities, there are numerous accommodation options close by, including cosy B&Bs, charming guest houses, hotels, and caravan parks with camping facilities.

Jenyns Circuit

21 Cedar Creek Falls

In the middle of a tall eucalypt forest, a well-constructed bitumen pathway leads you to a wonderful waterfall and a series of rock pools. There are gorge-like rock walls and towering trees, and the first section of this walk is suitable for strollers and wheelchairs. The starting point is a good spot for a picnic or BBQ.

At a glance

Grade: Medium
Time: 30 mins
Distance: 1 km return
Conditions: Partly shaded

Getting there

Car: Small parking area at the end of Cedar Creek Falls Road, off Tamborine Mountain Road

Cedar Creek Falls

21 Cedar Creek Falls

Walk directions

1 The walk begins at the end of the car park where there are interpretive signs. From here there is a bitumen path suitable for strollers and wheelchairs. Pass the first picnic area on the left. There are toilet facilities and the picnic areas are well-equipped with tables and BBQs.

2 Follow the track as it heads gently downhill and after a few minutes you reach a bridge. Straight ahead is a second picnic area. Turn left to follow the track over the bridge.

3 After a short distance, the first lookout point has views of the falls and water cascading over the rocks to the pools below. The tall trees stretch from the valleys below and compete with each other for the light above. High up on the other side of the valley are areas of erosion where control measures have been built. (The track beyond this point is not suitable for strollers or wheelchairs as it gets steeper and there are bush rock steps.) Continue on ahead towards the rock pools below.

4 In less than 50 metres the track branches. Take the left turn, continue downhill and descend a set of rock steps. It's worth stopping occasionally on the steps for views of the falls and, as you get closer, the rock pools. The

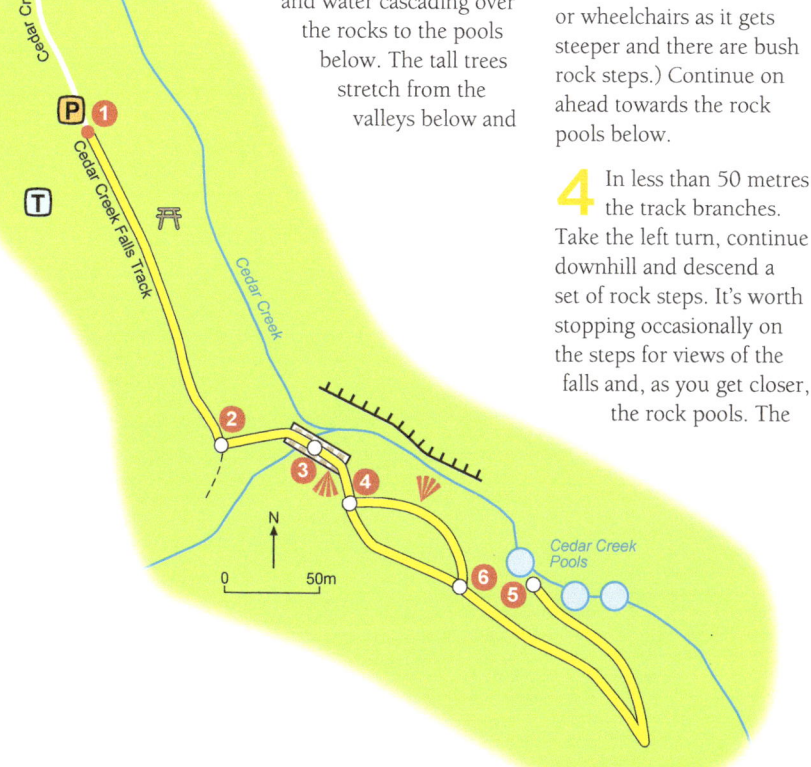

103

21 Cedar Creek Falls

track zigzags downhill and is fenced much of the way. Notice where the two branches of the track join as you'll be returning on the other track.

5 After about 500 metres you come to the rock pools. Be aware of the various warning signs in this area. The rocks here can be very slippery, particularly if they are wet. This scenic area is a good spot to rest before making the return journey.

6 Retrace your steps for about 500 metres. When you reach the fork in the path, take the left-hand track. Eventually you will come to another fork in the track (waypoint 4). Continue straight ahead to the lookout and then follow the path to the car park.

Lookout

21 Cedar Creek Falls

Cedar Creek

Tamborine Mountain – History

When Europeans first came in search of valuable timbers in the rainforests which originally covered Tamborine Mountain, the area was home to the Wangerriburras people. The first settlers arrived in 1875 after the land was opened for selection. The first of these was John O'Callaghan and his nephew E H O'Callaghan. Other early settlers were the Curtis Brothers who had a sawmill on the creek above Curtis Falls, which is named after them. The timber cutters were followed by farmers who cleared the forest to farm the rich volcanic soils. The area became a major farming and dairying area, and today is a significant horticultural production district. The early settlers also had the foresight to protect areas of rainforest and their efforts resulted in Witches Falls becoming Queensland's first national park in 1908.

22 Jenyns Circuit

Even in the middle of the day, the rainforest in this section of the Tamborine National Park can be quiet, dark and cool before it opens out into eucalypt forest. There are glimpses of the Gold Coast and the Pacific Ocean beyond.

Picabeen palms

At a glance

Grade: Medium
Time: 2 hrs
Distance: 5 km circuit
Conditions: Shady

Getting there

Car: Parking at Tamborine National Park entrance at the end of Palm Grove Avenue, off Eagle Heights Road, Tamborine

22 Jenyns Circuit

Walk directions

1 Begin at the entrance to the Palm Grove Section of the Tamborine National Park in Palm Grove Avenue, off Eagle Heights Road. Find the interpretive signs and pass through the stone-pillared gateway into the quiet and cool of the rainforest. The many signs along the track provide information on rainforest flora and fauna. The track can be quite muddy and slippery after rain and is rocky in places as you head downhill.

2 Some 450 metres into the park you'll find a turn-off to Curtis Road. Don't take this track, but instead stay to the left. You'll see stands of piccabeen palms which have tall straight stems that are slightly swollen at the base. A further 350 metres along is a sign explaining the buttressed root systems of the large trees and their grip on the earth. Continue on downhill to a fork in the track.

3 Take the right-hand path on the Jenyns Circuit Track. About 500 metres further on, still going gently downhill, the vegetation starts to change as more light enters the forest and you pass from the rainforest into the open eucalypt forest. Here there are stands of brush box, grey gum and hoop pine and this is a good area for wildlife spotting. There are some steep sides to the track here, so children will need to be closely supervised. The steepest sections have been fenced. After a descent of around 100 metres, the track starts to level out.

4 Continue on to meet a turn-off to the right marked *Jenyns Falls 365 metres* (closed at the time of writing). However, don't take this track but continue on a little way, to cross the creek. You may be able to hear the falls. Nearby are some excellent examples of strangler fig trees with their roots circling and enclosing the trunks of other species. Through the trees are glimpses of the Gold Coast in the distance. As the track starts to head uphill, keep an eye open for the effects of fire in the forest with large burnt-out tree stumps.

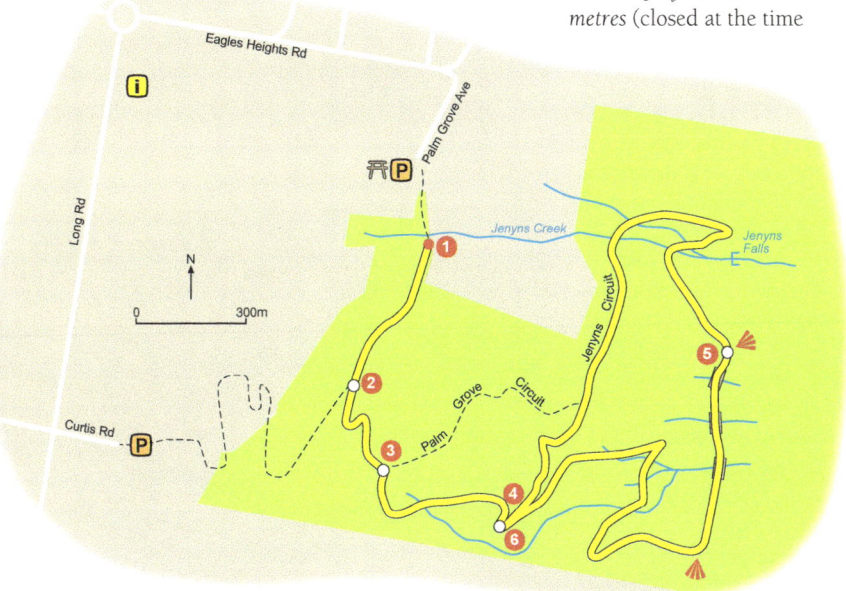

22 Jenyns Circuit

5 As the track turns back into the forest, pass by the turn-off to Burrawang Lookout (closed at the time of writing) which is on the right and up stone steps about 50 metres away. The burrawang is an ancient, slow-growing member of a small group of plants called the cycads. Continue on the main track.

6 At the next fork in the track, keep to the left and follow the signs to the car park and picnic area. From here, stay with the main track, ignoring turn-offs to other track entrances until you return to waypoint 3. From here, follow the signs to Palm Grove Avenue and the intersection where you started the circuit walk. The track continues uphill to the entrance through the rainforest and palm groves. Be sure to check for any wildlife that may have joined you, such as ticks and leeches.

22 Jenyns Circuit

Picabeen palms

Australian environment – Burrawang palm

The burrawang palm is not a true palm but an ancient, slow-growing member of a group of plants called the cycads. Fossil records indicate that they may have existed for up to 300 million years. There is an area on the mountain devoted to the cycads, called Zamia Grove, and this can be found on the Main Western Road past Witches Falls. However, on the Jenyns Circuit at Burrawang Lookout there are examples along the track starting near the steps to the lookout. They have long slender fronds in an attractive dark green colour, and the short trunks are rich in starch. Burrawang palms are sometimes used in landscaping, however the plant's bright red seeds are toxic to humans and animals.

23 Cameron Falls and Sandy Creek

Beginning just a short distance from the coffee shops in the centre of North Tamborine, this walk has panoramic views and explores towering Cameron Falls and the area's lush rainforest. This circuit track is in what is referred to as The Knoll section of Tamborine National Park.

At a glance

Grade: Medium
Time: 1 hr
Distance: 2.5 km circuit
Conditions: Shady

Getting there

Car: Limited parking at the end of Knoll Road, just beyond the end of Main Street, North Tamborine

23 Cameron Falls and Sandy Creek

Walk directions

1 Begin at the far end of the picnic area off Knoll Road, North Tamborine. There are magnificent views from the lookout, and even on a cloudy day you may get picturesque misty views. Begin following the dirt walking track which is just to the left as you enter the picnic area.

2 Follow the track as it descends steadily downhill into thick rainforest where you'll see large strangler fig trees. Along the way are mosses and ferns, native gingers and cordylines. There are a couple of little bridges over the track. Be careful as these can be slippery when wet.

View over Cameron Falls

23 Cameron Falls and Sandy Creek

3 Soon you'll come to the Sandy Creek Circuit Track which is 1.4 km long. Take the left turn to head to Cameron Falls. Near the creek are tall stands of piccabeen palms. At some stages of the year you will see the bright red fruits of the palms on the ground offering a stark contrast to the green vegetation. This part of the track can be quite muddy after rain.

4 You'll soon cross over the first of several bridges and some steps as you follow Sandy Creek. Notice how, as you approach the escarpment, the forest gets lighter with more plants in the lower storey.

5 As you emerge from the forest onto the falls escarpment, turn left and follow the track for 75 metres to Cameron Falls Lookout. There are views of the falls and surrounding countryside to the north and east towards Brisbane and Moreton Bay. Retrace your steps back to the main track and head straight ahead to continue on the circuit.

6 The track heads uphill and you'll encounter some more steps. On the more open escarpment areas are some introduced plants such as lantana which have become problem weeds in many national parks. Look out for name plates on some of the large trees. Many of these are valuable timber species which brought the first Europeans to the area.

7 Look out for some rocky areas as you continue uphill. There is evidence that tall trees have fallen, allowing light onto the forest floor. You may see changes in the vegetation close by. Many rainforest trees have large buttressed root systems and these often have cave-like structures in the base. You'll soon return to the beginning of the circuit track (waypoint 3). Turn left and follow the track up to the car park and picnic area.

Out and about – Exploring the rainforest with children

A rainforest is full of interesting things for children to look at and listen to. Set a challenge to count the number of different sounds that can be heard from the track: running water, birds, insects, animals moving about, wind in the treetops or water dripping off leaves. Find leaves that have a variety of shapes. Can you find a triangle, circle or spiky shape? Are there some leaves that are bigger than a child's head? What's the smallest leaf you can see? Although it might seem so at first glance, not everything in a rainforest is green – in fact, there's a surprising diversity of colour. Try bringing along a paint chart (free from hardware shops) and tick off the colours that can be seen during the walk. Older children often enjoy recording the family's walk with a digital camera.

23 Cameron Falls and Sandy Creek

A photographers paradise

113

24 MacDonald Rainforest Circuit

Just a short distance from the galleries, craft shops and cafés of Mt Tamborine's main street is a quiet, relaxing walk through a rainforest. While many of the walks on the mountain have steep sections, this is one of the gentlest with a reasonably flat path. The track explores a small pocket of land which was donated by Miss Jessie MacDonald in the 1930s and is popular with birdwatchers. Look out for spectacular strangler figs and lush palms.

At a glance

Grade: Easy
Time: 30 mins
Distance: 1.5 km circuit
Conditions: Shady

Getting there

Car: Follow Tamborine Mountain Road to Eagle Heights Road and at the next roundabout take Long Road to the left and follow to Wongawallan Road on the right. Limited parking on Wongawallan Road

Strangler figs

24 MacDonald Rainforest Circuit

Walk directions

1 Begin at the car park on Wongawallan Road off the main Tamborine Oxenford Road. The track starts off as bitumen but quickly becomes a dirt track which in wet weather or after rain can become very muddy. However, that is the normal rainforest environment – wet, dark, cool and humid. Continue on for about 250 metres.

2 At the intersection marking the beginning of the circuit track, turn left and continue on. This area is a good example of typical rainforest: there are tall, straight trees with large, shiny leaves and, closer to the ground, ferns, mosses and creepers. There are also some good examples of strangler figs. The remains of the original host tree that has been 'strangled' is often visible behind the fig's buttress roots. The extensive root

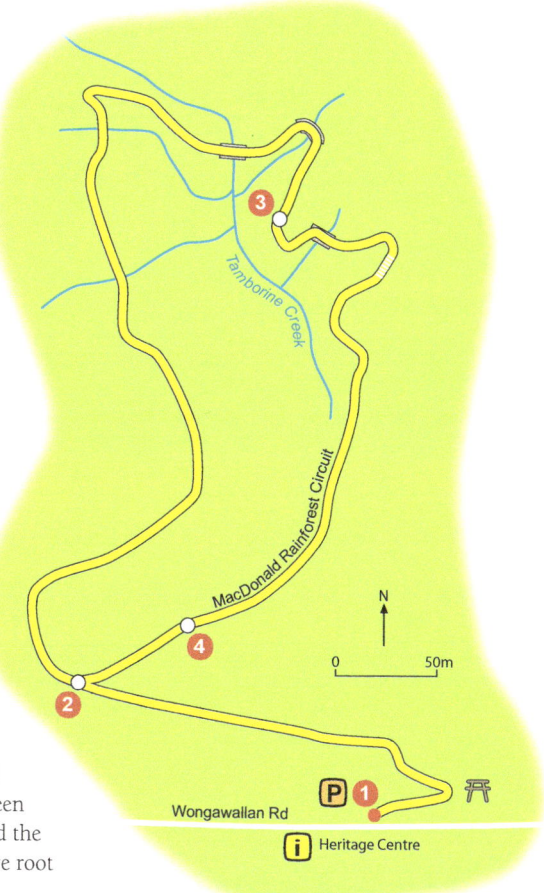

24 MacDonald Rainforest Circuit

system provides the trees with stability in the shallow rainforest soils. There is abundant birdlife in the rainforest and standing quietly for a few minutes may allow you to identify many different types of birdcall. While most birds are shy, some of the more curious species may fly in for a closer look at you if you stand still.

3 After about 15 minutes the track begins a gentle ascent again and there are several sets of steps. Keep an eye out for the tall trunks of piccabeen palms, a common feature of the creek walks on Tamborine. They grow to 25 metres and when fruiting, produce a bright red berry. Rainbow lorikeets and flying foxes feed on the flower's nectar.

4 After a few minutes, there are some more strangler figs. A glance up into the canopy may reveal other typical rainforest species including staghorns which perch high on the sides of tall trees. At the track junction (waypoint 2) take the left turn back to the car park along the same track you started down.

24 MacDonald Rainforest Circuit

Strangler fig

Australian environment – Strangler fig tree

The MacDonald section of Tamborine National Park was named after Miss Jessie MacDonald, who generously donated the land in the 1930s. It is this sort of foresight which allows us to enjoy the area today and particularly the magnificent strangler fig trees. The strangler fig or *Ficus watkinsiana* is a regular feature of the rainforests of South-East Queensland and can grow up to 45 metres tall. What is different about this tree is that it starts life high in the canopy. The tree's fruit is eaten by birds and tree-dwelling animals and the seeds are deposited high up in the crown of another tree. From here the seed germinates and sends long thin roots down to the floor of the rainforest. Once the roots reach the ground they form substantial buttresses. Slowly, over time, the fig competes with the host tree which may die and rot away. This can lead to quite spectacular hollow trunks where you can look up through the trunk and occasionally see as far as the sky and forest above.

25 Witches Falls Circuit

Turn back the hands of time as you walk in Queensland's very first national park, Witches Falls. This delightful circuit track takes in views over the mountains and farming country to the west as you descend into the rainforest below and visit the lookout to Witches Falls on a side track.

Views to the west

At a glance

Grade: Medium
Time: 1 hr
Distance: 3 km circuit
Conditions: Some shade

Getting there

Car: Follow Tamborine Mountain Road to Geissmann Drive and Main Western Road. About 1.5 km passed the Information Centre on the left is parking on Main Western Road adjacent to the National Park

25 Witches Falls Circuit

Walk directions

1 The track begins just beyond the memorial shelter to Queensland's first national park off Main Western Road. Turn left and follow the bitumen path as it zigzags downhill. The bitumen quickly gives way to a gravel path. There are views over to the distant ranges across farmlands.

2 As you enter the palm grove about 400 metres along the track, there are some stone steps. Look out for an alternative wet weather track which you may need to use if there has been a lot of rain. This section of the track gets very wet as you pass a series of lagoons surrounded by dense stands of piccabeen palms.

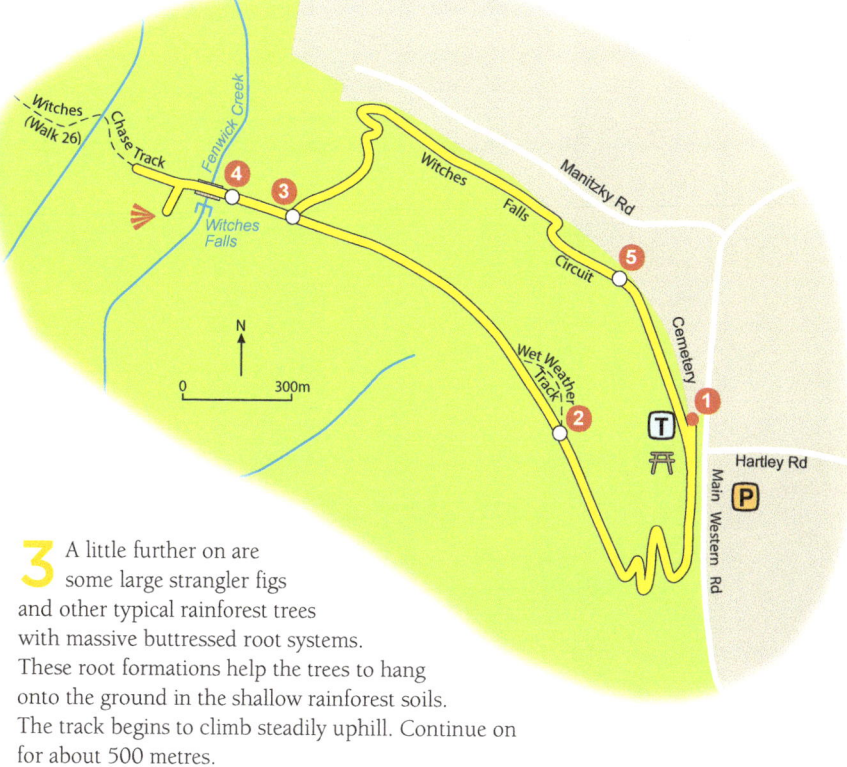

3 A little further on are some large strangler figs and other typical rainforest trees with massive buttressed root systems. These root formations help the trees to hang onto the ground in the shallow rainforest soils. The track begins to climb steadily uphill. Continue on for about 500 metres.

4 Look out for a side track with a sign indicating that it is 200 metres to Witches Falls Lookout. Follow this side track and you'll cross a small bridge just before the lookout which has a fenced platform. The falls are most impressive if there has been recent rain. The track past the falls leads to Witches Chase Road (see Walk 26).

25 Witches Falls Circuit

5 Retrace your steps back to the main track and turn left uphill and up some rocky steps. Follow the track until it levels out and passes some houses on the left. As you emerge from the forest, there is a cemetery to the left. This is an interesting place to explore in order to get a glimpse of the area's former residents. A little further on are interpretive displays on the park, its inhabitants, forest and history. Continue on to your starting point.

25 Witches Falls Circuit

Australian history – Queensland's first national park

The world's first national park was established at Yellowstone in the USA in 1872 and the second was what is now called the Royal National Park in Sydney later in 1872. However, for Queensland it all started on Mount Tamborine where the Witches Falls National Park was proclaimed on 28 March 1908. It was the foresight of local shire councillors Sydney Curtis and J H Delpratt, who had concerns about the level of tree clearing in the area, that led to the creation of the national park. This was followed over the years by further additions that now encompass some fourteen areas totalling over 3000 hectares in the Tamborine area under a number of different land tenures. Today Queensland has a network of over 150 national parks stretching from Cape York in the north to the New South Wales border in the south, and west to the Simpson Desert National Park in South-West Queensland. At first, national parks were set aside for recreational use, but today they are carefully managed to not only provide recreation, but also to preserve a variety of landscapes and the biodiversity of our unique flora and fauna.

26 Witches Chase

With views of mountains and farming lands, the first part of this track, which traverses the western side of a ridge through tall timbers, offers a secluded and peaceful rainforest experience. However, the second section presents the opportunity to visit a local winery, art gallery and quirky distillery which uses locally grown fruit to produce liqueurs.

At a glance

Grade: Medium
Time: 2 hrs
Distance: 5.5 km circuit
Conditions: Some shade

Getting there

Car: From the Main Western Road just past the Information Centre take Beacon Road for about 1 km to Witches Chase. Parking at Witches Chase off Beacon Road

Farming lands to the west

26 Witches Chase

Walk directions

1 Begin at the end of the wonderfully named Witches Chase, off a sharp bend in Beacon Road. The track entrance is marked by two stone and concrete cairns and heads gently downhill through open forest which quickly turns to rainforest.

2 As you enter the forest, the wide dirt track quickly narrows and there are bush steps made from local rock as you continue downhill. Take care, as some parts of the track become quite rocky and uneven underfoot. As you continue along the track, there are views to the west, over the surrounding countryside. The palms with tall, straight trunks are piccabeen palms which are common in the local area. Also keep an eye out for strangler figs which can grow to 45 metres.

3 After about 1.5 kilometres, follow a small side track to the right, which leads to the Witches Falls Lookout. After taking in the view, retrace your steps to the main track.

Buttressed roots

Australian rainforest environment – Buttress roots

Many of the tall rainforest trees have buttress roots around their base. In rainforest soils, most of the nutrients are in the upper layers. Additionally, many rainforest soils are shallow and large trees need to develop a substantial root system to prevent them from falling over. As the roots spread out, often for many metres from the tree, they gather nutrients and intertwine with the roots of other trees. The exposed roots of fallen trees provide a glimpse of the network of roots and the depth to which they have penetrated the rainforest soils.

26 Witches Chase

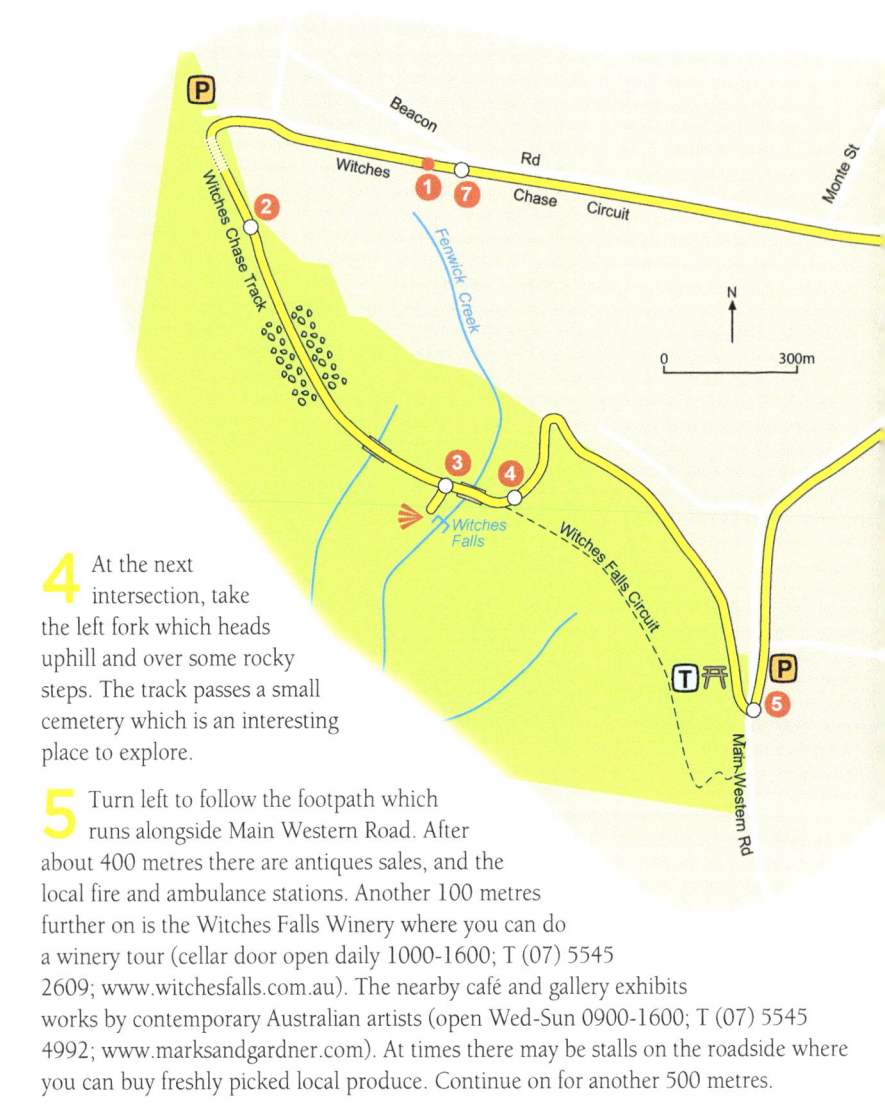

4 At the next intersection, take the left fork which heads uphill and over some rocky steps. The track passes a small cemetery which is an interesting place to explore.

5 Turn left to follow the footpath which runs alongside Main Western Road. After about 400 metres there are antiques sales, and the local fire and ambulance stations. Another 100 metres further on is the Witches Falls Winery where you can do a winery tour (cellar door open daily 1000-1600; T (07) 5545 2609; www.witchesfalls.com.au). The nearby café and gallery exhibits works by contemporary Australian artists (open Wed-Sun 0900-1600; T (07) 5545 4992; www.marksandgardner.com). At times there may be stalls on the roadside where you can buy freshly picked local produce. Continue on for another 500 metres.

6 Before turning left into Beacon Road you may like to visit the local Information Centre (open daily 1000-1530) which is just ahead in Doughty Park. Return to Beacon Road and follow the concrete footpath beside it, passing the local Tamborine Bowling Club and swimming pool.

7 After about 800 metres, on the opposite side of the road, you'll see the ornate gates of the Tamborine Mountain Distillery which produces unusual and award-winning products such as Lemon Myrtle Leaf Vodka and Passionfruit Liqueur (open Mon-Sat 1000-1500; T (07) 5545 l3452; www.tamborinemountaindistillery.com). After a further 200 metres, take the left fork into Witches Chase Road and return to the start of the walk.

26 Witches Chase

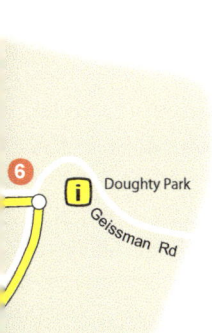

Doughty Park
Geissman Rd

Staghorns

27 Curtis Falls

Rock-hopping skills are needed on this walk, which crosses pretty Cedar Creek a number of times. There are stands of piccabeen palms in the lush rainforest and close-up views of the resident flying fox colony. If you're short of time, there is a 1-kilometre return walk to Curtis Falls, however the circuit section of this walk is quieter, and you're likely to spot some local wildlife.

Cedar Creek

At a glance

Grade: Medium
Time: 1 hr 30 mins
Distance: 3.5 km return
Conditions: Shady

Getting there

Car: Parking near the start of the track in Dapsang Drive, Mount Tamborine

27 Curtis Falls

Walk directions

1 Begin at the entrance to the Joalah section of the national park adjacent to the car park in Dapsang Drive. 'Joalah' is an Aboriginal word meaning 'haunt of the lyrebird'. Follow the track as it heads gently downhill through eucalypt forest and then into the cool of the rainforest. The track just inside the park, heading off to the left, is a 200-metre pathway which leads to the cafés on Eagle Heights Road. However, ignore this path and continue on the main track for 300 metres.

2 Look out for a track to the left for a short side trip to a wooden landing and seats. There is a view of the track below through the rainforest. Tall, straight trees compete for light with an array of other rainforest plants. Crow's nest and staghorn ferns cling to the trunks of trees, often high up in the canopy of the forest. Retrace your steps to the main track which continues downhill and involves some steps.

3 Another 250 metres along is a turn-off to the left signed *Curtis Falls 105 metres*. Follow this track to the base of the falls where the water cascades into a pool and is particularly spectacular after heavy rain. This is the headwaters of Cedar Creek which is crossed several times during this walk.

4 Return to the main track and take the turn to *Lower Creek Circuit 2.4 km*. The track continues downhill through lush rainforest and tall stands of piccabeen palms. The palms are home to a colony of noisy flying foxes which live high up in the canopy. You may notice the smell of the colony. Avoid contact with the flying foxes for health reasons. Continue along the track following the signs.

5 Follow the track to the right as it

127

27 Curtis Falls

crosses the creek. Take care here as the walking surface becomes more challenging and can be slippery. Keep a sharp eye out for any wildlife such as water dragons – a water dragon is a lizard that is often found near creeks. Continue on to the next creek crossing, where some rock-hopping skills are needed. Be careful as it can be very slippery.

6 After crossing the creek there are about 50 rock steps as you start to head uphill. Way above you, you'll get glimpses of the armour guardrail on the road above and you start to hear the traffic noise. The track now climbs well above the creek for a short distance before descending again to the water.

7 When you reach a small bridge, follow the creek uphill. The road is just above and you have completed the lower circuit of the walk. Continue on the track back towards Curtis Falls Lookout then retrace your steps back to the car park.

Walk variation

If you'd prefer a short but pretty walk before enjoying coffee and cake at the Eagle Heights Road cafés, take the 400-metre side track which joins the 1-kilometre return path to Curtis Falls Lookout.

27 Curtis Falls

Australian rainforest environment – Three very different palms

There are many palms in the rainforest, particularly along creek walks. Palms are unique in that their growing point is at the top or apex of the tree. One of the most common palms, *Archontophoenix cunninghamiana*, is known as the piccabeen palm in Queensland and the Bangalow palm in northern New South Wales. This is a medium to tall palm with a straight cylindrical trunk, slightly swollen at the base, which grows to 25 metres. It bears small, bright red, berry-like fruit and the fruit and flowers attract a wide range of birds and the grey-headed flying fox. A much finer and smaller species, only about 3 metres tall, is the walking stick palm, *Linospadix monostachya*. It takes its common name from its appearance, as it resembles a walking stick. The third palm is *Calamus muelleri* known as lawyer vine or wait-a-while. The latter is an appropriate name as this palm is a climber with sharp thin spines which help it climb high into the forest canopy, but also catch onto walkers' clothes, skin and packs. As soon as you untangle yourself from one hook, another can attach itself and you have to 'wait a while'.

Flying foxes

Purling Brook Falls

Hinterland South – Springbrook

Springbrook, a beautiful area in the mountains at the southern end of the Gold Coast, is just 30 km from Mudgeeraba. The drive there is along a picturesque and winding mountain road. This is a land of towering trees with a mix of eucalypt forest, rainforest and magnificent waterfalls. From the lookouts there are sweeping views to the coast. This is a wonderful place for a quiet day in the bush, although you may find many others with similar plans on weekends and during holiday periods. While Springbrook is less developed than the other hinterland area of Tamborine, there are still a few cafés and restaurants, picnic areas and a range of walks, from easy strolls to harder walks for the fitter and more experienced walker. The Springbrook National Park has camping facilities and there are other accommodation options close by including B&Bs, farm stays and guest houses.

Eastern escarpment

28 Springbrook Warrie Circuit

This is the longest and most challenging track in the Springbrook National Park. Walkers require a reasonable level of fitness and need to have suitable bushwalking equipment. Caution needs to be exercised on slippery surfaces, near cliffs and at creek crossings which can be difficult after rain. The track follows the cliff edge and care is needed, particularly with children, as one slip could be fatal. Keep a sharp eye out for snakes and, in wet areas, leeches. It takes about 10 km to descend 400 m to the Meeting of the Waters before winding uphill back to the start. It is, however, a scenic, well-signposted track with many waterfalls. In fact, the name Warrie is Aboriginal for rushing waters. The Department of Environment and Resource Management website has more information: visit www.nprsr.qld.gov.au and do a search in the top right-hand corner for 'Springbrook'.

At a glance

Grade: Hard
Time: 6 hrs
Distance: 17 km circuit
Conditions: Partly shady and slippery after rain with many creek crossings

Getting there

Car: Travel to Springbrook from the Gold Coast Highway. Pass the Information Centre and school and continue on for 4.5 km to Tallanbana picnic area

Rainbow Falls

28 Springbrook Warrie Circuit

Walk directions

1 Begin at the Tallanbana picnic area where there are parking and picnic facilities. The track leads off from the bottom of the picnic area and enters the rainforest. About 300 metres in is an intersection. Take the right-hand track to the Warrie Circuit. The track starts heading gently downhill almost straight away.

2 A further kilometre on is an intersection with the Twin Falls track. Continue to follow the signs to the Warrie Circuit. This is the last intersection with other tracks until you have the chance to rejoin the Twin Falls track near the end of the walk. A little further on is the first major waterfall, Rainbow Falls. The track, which can be very slippery, goes behind the falls.

3 A further 1.5 kilometres brings you down a steep slope, part of which is fenced, to Goomoolahara Falls.

Poonyahra Falls

Springbrook environment – Geology

The rugged escarpments of the Springbrook area are obvious on this walk and form part of the World Heritage area proclaimed over South-East Queensland's Scenic Rim in 1994. This includes the Lamington National Park to the west, Mt Barney National Park and parts of Main Range National Park even further west as well as parts of Northern New South Wales. The waterfalls on this track are part of the modern-day erosion cycle of the mountain and the source of many creeks which feed into the rivers flowing to the Gold Coast. The escarpments were created by the rhyolite and basalt lava flows from the ancient Tweed volcano. This volcano was centred on Mt Warning. The ranges and rocky outcrops on the Gold Coast and in the hinterland are the result of its extensive lava flows.

28 Springbrook Warrie Circuit

28 Springbrook Warrie Circuit

Continue downhill for another 3 kilometres, passing through patches of eucalypt forest before re-entering the rainforest. Along the way are numerous creek crossings, some of which can be difficult and slippery to negotiate.

4 The next major waterfall is Ngarri-dhum Falls. Continue downhill for another four kilometres through rainforest.

5 Look out for a short side track to the Meeting of the Waters where two creek systems join. Follow the side track and you'll see where the waters from Goomoolahra and Ngarri-dhum Falls meet as Mundora Creek. This creek joins Little Nerang Creek. This is a good spot for a rest break or picnic. From here, the track starts to head uphill.

6 You'll soon reach Gooroolba Falls. Continue on uphill. There are lots of switchbacks and the going can get tough at times, but there are plenty of opportunities to rest and observe the forest's plants and animals. In the wet areas there are often wonderful examples of colourful fungi.

7 Look out for a sign marking the side track to Poonyahra Falls. It's about 75 metres in and well worth a visit. Poonyahra means 'beautiful'. Return to the main track and on to Poondahra Falls. Continue on to the next signed track intersection and follow the track marked *To Canyon Lookout*, ignoring the Twin Falls track. After a sharp turn, the track levels out.

8 Continue on to Canyon Lookout. Across the road is Rosellas at Springbrook, a charming café housed in an historic homestead and generally open Fri-Sun (T 0427 335 384). The garden is often visited by colourful parrots called crimson rosellas. From here, follow the track to the sign which directs you back to Tallanbana picnic ground and your starting point.

29 Twin Falls Circuit

Walk along the picturesque escarpment with views to the coast before descending to walk along the base of the towering moss and fern-covered cliffs and behind spectacular waterfalls in the subtropical rainforest. The track then emerges from the forest as it climbs back to the top of the escarpment, passing more lookouts. After rain the track can be quite muddy and slippery, but enjoy the spray as you walk behind the falls.

At a glance

Grade: Medium
Time: 2 hrs
Distance: 4 km circuit
Conditions: Shaded

Getting there

Car: Take Boy-Ull Road off Springbrook Road, Springbrook. Park in Canyon Parade

29 Twin Falls Circuit

Walk directions

1 Start at Canyon Lookout, adjacent to the car park, and after taking in the views to the Gold Coast take the track to the right. You'll walk in an anticlockwise direction along the escarpment, passing through open eucalypt scrub on poorer soils. This path has some steps.

2 The next lookout is called Tallaringa, meaning 'over the trees'. A small concrete bridge crosses a creek which plunges over the escarpment to become Tallanbana waterfall. Just beyond is Ballaringa Lookout and a sign explaining the many Aboriginal names and meanings in the area.

3 Half a kilometre from the start, you arrive at a track junction. Ignore the path to Tallanbana picnic area and take the left-hand track which leads to Twin Falls Circuit. There are some steps on this downhill track.

4 Cross the small bridge over the top of Tamarramai Falls and continue downwards through a series of switchbacks. As you descend towards the base of the cliff, you'll pass through narrow openings between large rock surfaces.

5 At the next intersection, take the Twin Falls Circuit track to the left. The other track is to the Warrie Circuit, a much longer and harder walk (see Walk 28).

6 At the next intersection, go left again and follow the base of the escarpment. There are interesting interpretive signs about the forest and its inhabitants.

137

29 Twin Falls Circuit

7 At a branch in the track take the upper, left-hand path and walk behind the cascading waters of Twin Falls. (It's possible to take the right-hand track which passes over a concrete causeway in front of the falls if you're concerned about getting wet.) Continue on, passing towering cliffs covered in ferns, mosses and lichens, and tall rainforest trees.

8 Look out for the short side track which takes you to a cave in the rocks. Retrace your steps to the main track and a little further on is a large rock overhang. Keep an eye out for local birdlife including the green catbird, scrub turkey, eastern yellow robin and the rarer Albert's lyrebird.

9 At the next intersection turn left. You'll soon come to Blackfellow Falls and the track goes behind the waterfall. Begin heading uphill to cross the creek at the top and then along the escarpment. The track leaves the rainforest behind and enters the eucalypt forest on the poorer and shallow rhyolitic-derived soils. You'll see xanthorrhoea plants, also called grass trees, the resin from which was used by Aborigines for weapon making. The track is now more open and passes several lookouts before arriving back at Canyon Lookout.

Twin Falls

Canyon lookout

138

29 Twin Falls Circuit

Australian environment – Lichens

Rocks quickly become discoloured in nature with exposure to light, water and air, along with colonisation of their surfaces by plant life. In rainforests you'll see lichens colouring patches on rocks and trees. They can sometimes be a light grey-green colour, but lichens can also come in bright colours and have been used for making dyes. They are a fungus and algae which live happily together for their mutual benefit. Lichens break down the surfaces they are attached to and form organic matter in which larger lichens, mosses and eventually ferns can establish themselves. Where established on trees they'll be found on the southern side, away from direct sunlight.

30 Purling Brook Falls

The water at Purling Brook Falls tumbles more than a hundred metres over a massive cliff of volcanic rocks into the gorge below. This walk descends to the base of the falls where the track goes behind the waterfall. On the way you'll pass through subtropical rainforest with a myriad of different plants from tall trees to tiny ferns, accompanied by a chorus of rainforest birds.

At a glance

Grade: Medium
Time: 2 hrs
Distance: 4 km circuit
Conditions: Shaded

Getting there

Car: Parking at Gwongorella picnic area at the end of Forestry Road off the Gold Coast Springbrook Road, Springbrook

Purling Brook Falls

30 Purling Brook Falls

Walk directions

1 Begin at the end of the car park where there are interpretive signs. At the first intersection go left. There is a board explaining Indigenous names that apply to many features in the park. The track here is bitumen which soon gives way to a good dirt track. You'll pass a series of spots with good views of the falls, the valley below and the huge creamy-coloured rhyolite cliff over which the falls tumble. Rhyolite is a fine-grained, light-coloured volcanic rock. In the distance you can see the high-rise buildings on the coast. Down in the valley below is the lower section of the track.

2 The track heads downhill via numerous sets of steps and switchbacks. There are fenced sections of the track with warnings of unstable cliff edges. You'll pass numerous burrawang plants, the ancient cycads, which are known from fossil records from 300 million years ago. Continue to follow the track which takes about 400 steps to the bottom of the falls.

Basalt Cliffs

Gold Coast environment – Look after our parks

When you visit and enjoy our national parks you have a very important role to play in their future. Be sure not to pick, damage or collect any plants or disturb animals, and take your rubbish with you when you leave. Food scraps left in parks can harm native animals. It is also important to ensure your equipment, particularly boots, clothes, backpacks and even your car are clean when entering parks. A very new and serious threat to our bushlands is myrtle rust, which was first found in Australia in 2010. It is a serious fungal disease that affects plants in the Myrtaceae family. This includes many Australian natives like bottlebrush, tea-tree, lilly pillies and eucalypts.

30 Purling Brook Falls

3 After a steady half-hour walk, at a junction, take the track to Warringa Pool. Follow the path downhill for 20 minutes.

4 You'll see a large basalt rock slab surrounding Warringa Pool, a picturesque waterhole. Basalt is a dark grey or black fine-grained rock you will also encounter elsewhere on the walk, and is the result of lava flows. This is a good place for a rest and a snack. Retrace your steps back uphill to rejoin the main track at waypoint 3.

5 Continue on to the left for a couple of minutes until you reach Purling Brook Falls, where the path hugs the cliff and goes behind the waterfall. Keep an eye out for water dragons, large lizards that like to sun themselves on rocks. You'll see dark basalt rock layers in the lower areas under the rhyolite cliffs. The track climbs steadily up the opposite side of the gorge with numerous steps and frequent switchbacks. There are views across the gorge and you can see the lookouts on the other side which you visited earlier.

6 As you reach the top, take a 100-metre detour to a lookout over Purling Brook Falls. Retrace your steps and follow the path across the creek at the top of the falls. The track is now sealed. After a few hundred metres you'll come to the intersection at the start of the track. Turn left to the car park.

30 Purling Brook Falls

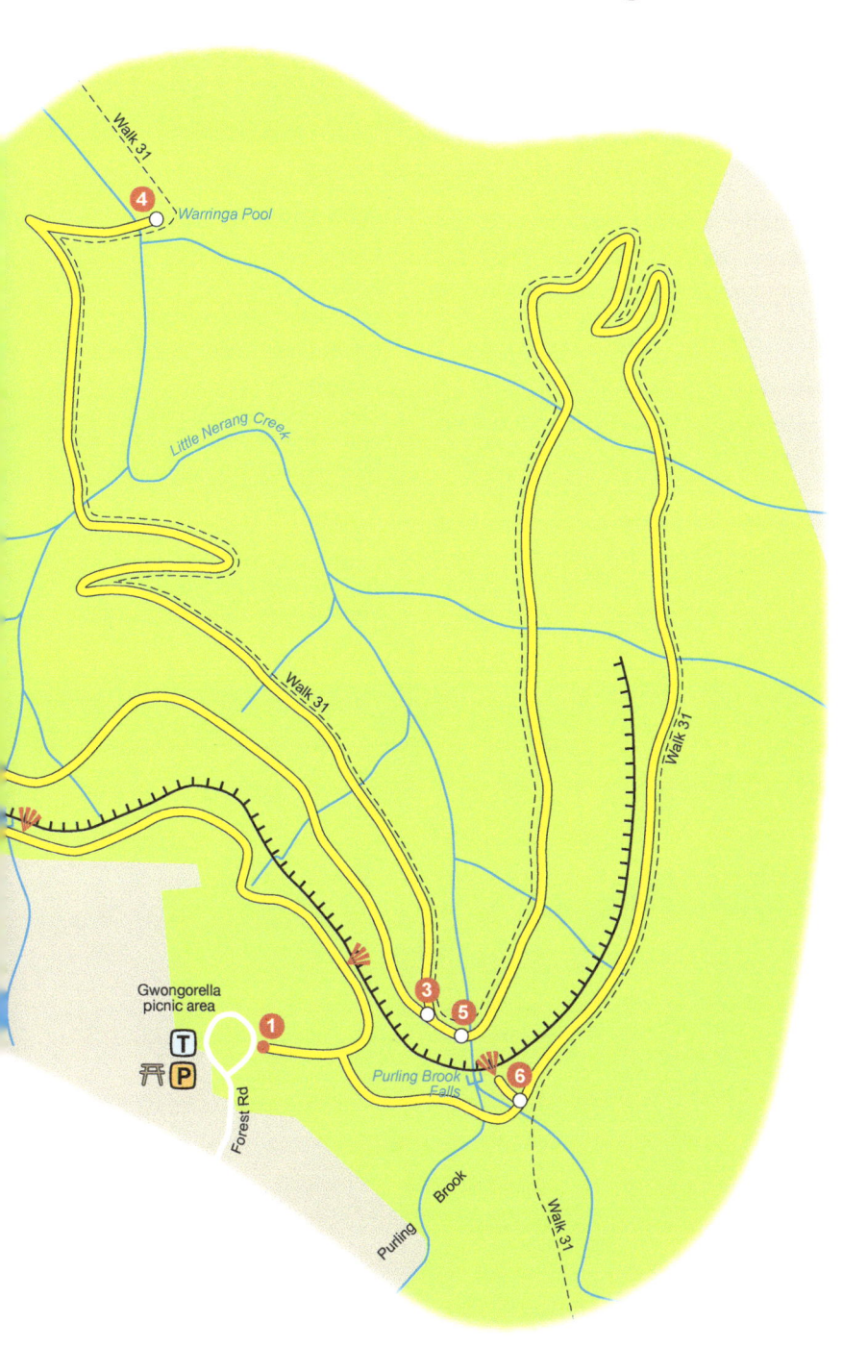

31 Apple Tree Park to Settlement Day Use Area

Part of the Gold Coast Hinterland Great Walk linking the Woonoongoora walkers' camp to Purling Brook Falls, this walk passes through magnificent forests. It does, however, involve crossing streams which can be difficult after rain. Walkers should obtain the Gold Coast Hinterland Great Walks topographic map which is available from the Department of National Parks Recreation, Sport and Racing Customer Referral Centre (T 13 74 68).

At a glance

Grade: Hard
Time: 3 hrs
Distance: 7 km one way
Conditions: Shaded
Getting there
Car: Car shuffle required for this walk. Park at Apple Tree Park on Springbrook Road, Springbrook, 1 kilometre past Wunburra Lookout (nearest intersection is Pine Creek Road). Park the other car at The Settlement Day Use Area in Carricks Road, Springbrook

Warringa Pool

31 Apple Tree Park to Settlement Day Use Area

Walk directions

1 Begin at Apple Tree Park on the Springbrook Road, 1 kilometre past Wunburra Lookout. Cross Springbrook Road and find the *Great Walks track* marking arrow. Follow the track a short distance to the dirt service road and turn right along the road. This is a powerline easement and you will see regular markers indicating an underground powerline. The large tree stumps are remnants of previous logging days. Some of these still show the rectangular holes cut by the timber getters for their springboards, which allowed them to climb the trees while cutting them by hand with axe and saw.

2 About 700 metres further on, follow the track as it heads uphill at a steeper grade. After another 250 metres continue on as the track turns left. Walk down to the gate which marks the entrance of the National Park.

3 Just inside the gate is a sign explaining that the track descends 245 metres, the equivalent of a 61-storey building. Head steeply downhill using many rock steps, as you leave the plateau and descend to Little Nerang Creek. This section can be slippery after rain. Along the way keep an eye out for wildlife, particularly birds. You may see tiny purple and white native violets along the edge of the track.

4 At the bottom, cross Little Nerang Creek with care as the rocks can be slippery and the water level will vary depending on recent rain. Pick up the track again, which has rock steps. In some places there is deep leaf litter and exposed tree roots. Follow the creek upstream for about 1 kilometre through heavy forest. There are cascading waters and rock pools in this narrow gorge.

5 You'll emerge at Warringa Pool where there are large basalt rock slabs. This a good place for a rest and to take the opportunity to enjoy the tranquillity of the forest. Head uphill along the track for another kilometre to join the Purling Brook Falls Circuit. Take the track which leads to the falls.

George Haddock Bridge

31 Apple Tree Park to Settlement Day Use Area

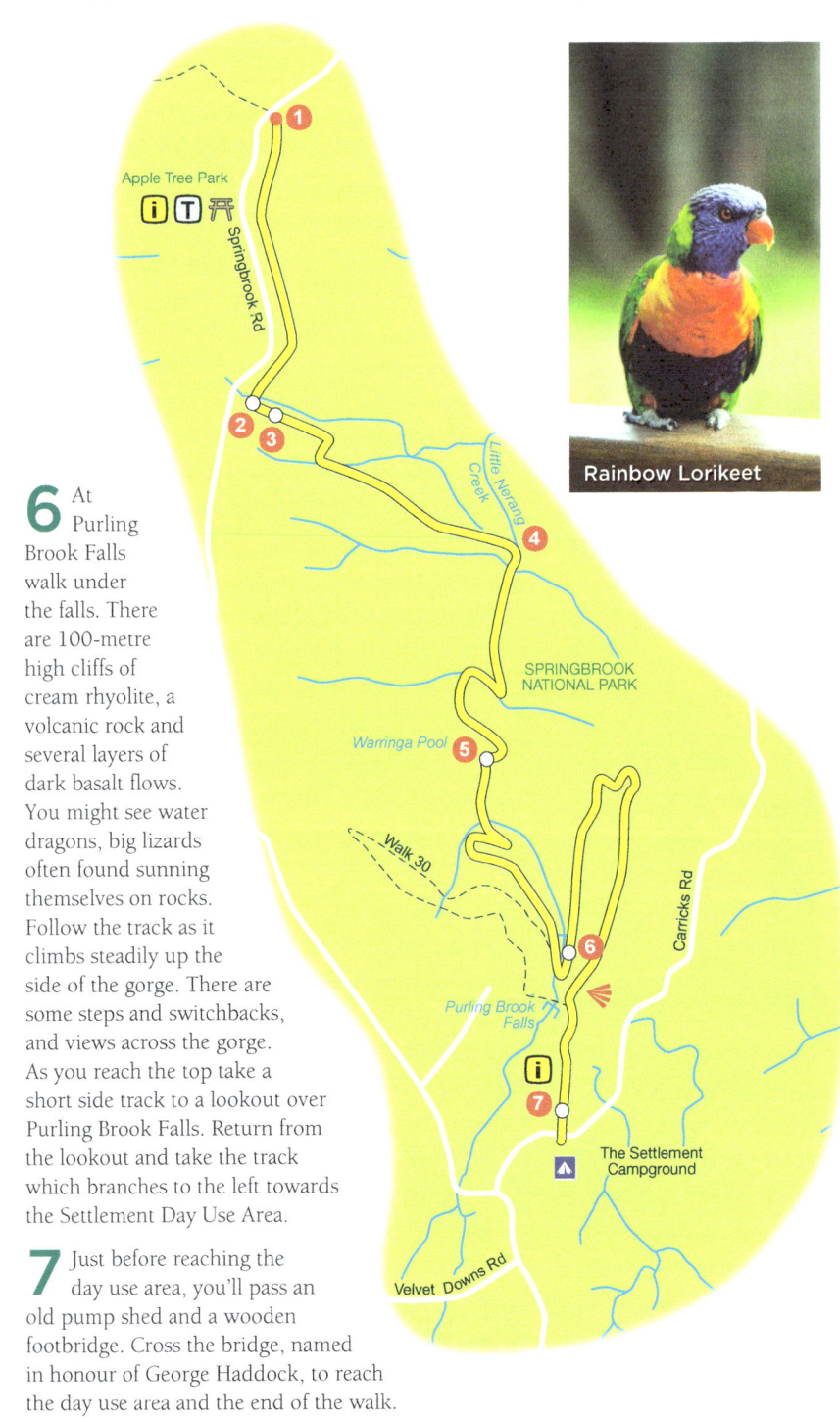

Rainbow Lorikeet

6 At Purling Brook Falls walk under the falls. There are 100-metre high cliffs of cream rhyolite, a volcanic rock and several layers of dark basalt flows. You might see water dragons, big lizards often found sunning themselves on rocks. Follow the track as it climbs steadily up the side of the gorge. There are some steps and switchbacks, and views across the gorge. As you reach the top take a short side track to a lookout over Purling Brook Falls. Return from the lookout and take the track which branches to the left towards the Settlement Day Use Area.

7 Just before reaching the day use area, you'll pass an old pump shed and a wooden footbridge. Cross the bridge, named in honour of George Haddock, to reach the day use area and the end of the walk.

31 Apple Tree Park to Settlement Day Use Area

Queensland environment – Great Walks

The Great Walks of Queensland explore some of the most magnificent and scenic natural areas of the State. The walks, of which there are currently ten, cross parts of most of the World Heritage listed sections of the State. While completing the whole walk usually takes days, most offer sections which can be covered in a day or half-day walk. The experiences range from tropical rainforests to sandy beaches, crystal clear freshwater lagoons to towering geological features, massive waterfalls and gorges, as well as the rich Indigenous culture and settlement history of the State and the world's largest sand island – Fraser Island. The 54 km Gold Coast Hinterland Walk starts out at Green Mountain in Lamington National Park and traverses the park via Binna Burra and the Numinbah Valley to the Springbrook National Park, ending at Purling Brook Falls track.

32 Natural Bridge

A spectacular natural rock bridge carved out over thousands of years by water is found in the rainforest on the western side of the Springbrook National Park. This short walk along a sealed pathway with many steps is spectacular both during the day and at night. At night the cave comes alive with millions of glow worms.

At a glance

Grade: Easy
Time: 1 hr
Distance: 1 km circuit
Conditions: Shaded

Getting there

Car: Parking on Bakers Road, off Nerang-Murwillumbah Road, Natural Bridge, 9 km past the Numinbah Correctional Centre

Natural Bridge

32 Natural Bridge

Walk directions

1 Begin in the car park and find the interpretive shelter. It's worth reading about the area and the formation of the bridge. Follow the signs that take you for a short walk down to the beginning of the track.

2 At the start of the circuit track take the path to the left to walk in a clockwise direction. On your left is a giant strangler fig tree. The sealed and fenced path heads downhill, and includes over eighty steps. Watch for interpretive signage and special trees which have been named. Continue following the path through the subtropical rainforest.

Hoop Pine

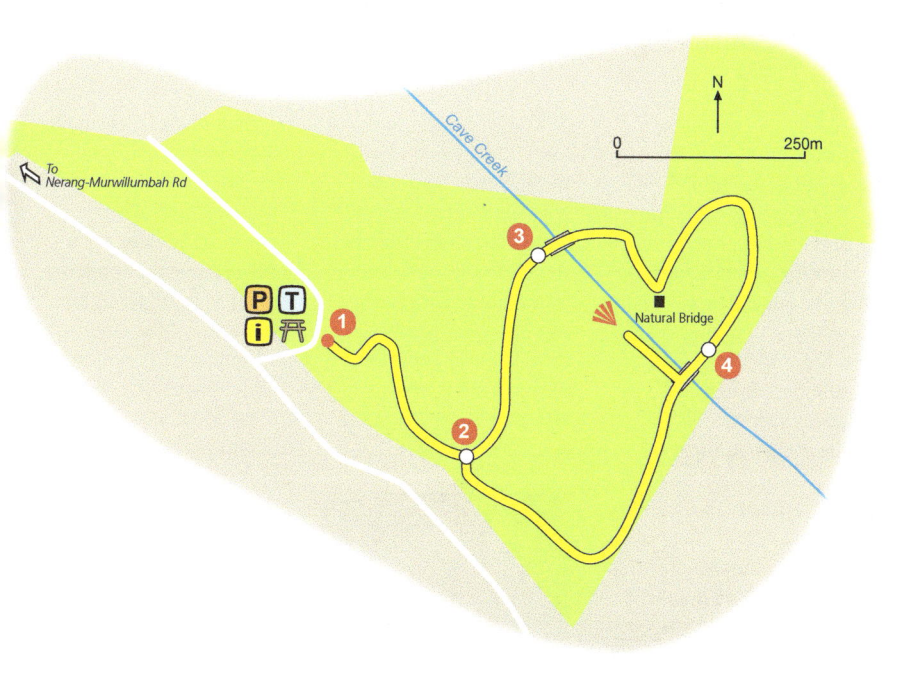

32 Natural Bridge

3 You'll reach Cave Creek. Cross the bridge and follow the path uphill to the natural rock bridge where there are about 30 steps up to the viewing point. Before you is the large rock arch with a waterfall tumbling through a hole into the pool below. Another 30 steps takes you down into the cave under the bridge. At night the area comes alive with the luminescence of the glow worms. Also on the ceiling are numerous small flying foxes. Retrace your steps back to the main track and continue following the path.

4 After crossing the next bridge, look out for a 50-metre-long side track to the right which leads to another viewing area. This is close to where the creek tumbles through to the pool below. Long ago the water would have tumbled over the edge of the basalt bridge as a waterfall but the swirling action of the water eventually eroded through the rock to create the hole. This action also created the cave below in the softer agglomerate rock. Return to the main track and continue on uphill to reach the strangler fig tree at the start of the circuit and waypoint 2. *Continue* uphill towards the end of the track passing a stand of hoop pines or *Araucaria cunninghamii*. The hoop pine is one of the world's ancient conifers, easily identified by its straight trunk and distinctive pine tree bark. Just ahead is the car park.

Native ginger

32 Natural Bridge

Queensland environment – Glow worms

The glow worm known as *Arachnocampa flava*, which is found in Queensland, is not a worm but an insect (or more correctly the larva or larviform female of an insect). Glow worms are bioluminescent, which is where the blue-green light comes from, and they are found in sheltered spots in the forest or in caves. This makes Natural Bridge a very suitable place for them. The larvae produce fine web-like threads which trap insects attracted to the luminescence in their tail. The catch is reeled in using the glow worm's mouthparts and stored. When present in large numbers glow worms make a spectacular night-time display.

Cascades into Natural Bridge pool

Walk variation

To see the glow worms, do the walk at night. Make sure you carry a good torch and take care negotiating the track in the dark. To get the best view, stand on the viewing platform and turn your torch off. At the entrance to the cave are instructions on what to do and what not to do: for example, do not smoke, and do not shine your torch on the glow worms or try to touch them.

33 Mount Cougal Cascades

There are few areas of cool, quiet rainforest close to the Gold Coast beaches. This one is just a 20 km drive west of Currumbin along Currumbin Creek Road, in the Mt Cougal section of the Springbrook National Park at the headwaters of Currumbin Creek. Take time to explore the environment and its history which is well signposted. Also along the way, 14 km from the Coast at the side of the road, are the Currumbin Rock Pools. It is amazing how quickly you leave behind the development of the Coast and enter the world of subtropical rainforest and the rocky creek bed. This can be a popular spot when the weather or conditions on the beach are poor. Note that although you are just 20 km from the Gold Coast, you may be outside of mobile phone range.

At a glance

Grade: Easy
Time: 1 hr
Distance: 1.5 km return
Conditions: Shady. Bitumen path. No dogs allowed.

Getting there

Car: Park at the start of the walking track, about 20 km drive west of Currumbin along Currumbin Creek Road in the Mt Cougal section of the Springbrook National Park

33 Mount Cougal Cascades

Walk directions

1 The track starts from the car park and heads gently uphill. There is a sign with information about the park and its wildlife. The track is well signed with interesting information about the flora and fauna, the Indigenous people and the history of the area. This is the home of the Yugambeh people.

2 You'll soon reach the first viewing platform from where you can see the waters of the creek cascading over the rocks. In places there are steps to allow you to get closer to the creek. If venturing onto the rocks, be very careful as they can be slippery and dangerous. Take note of the National Parks safety signs and notices. The rocks are part of the cycle of erosion in the area and are basalt and rhyolite lava flows from the former Tweed volcano. As you walk keep an eye out for scrub turkeys scratching on the forest floor and large lizards sunning themselves on the rocks beside the creek.

3 A little further on is a sign about how the area was once cleared and farmed – would you believe there were banana plantations in the area? (See 'Mt Cougal history' below/on page 155.) Land clearing for farming started in about 1920. Depending on the time of the day there can be an array of different birds. You may even hear whipbirds which sound a little like a stock whip being cracked. The call is actually produced by a male and female pair of birds making the sound together as a duet. They are sometimes seen but more often heard.

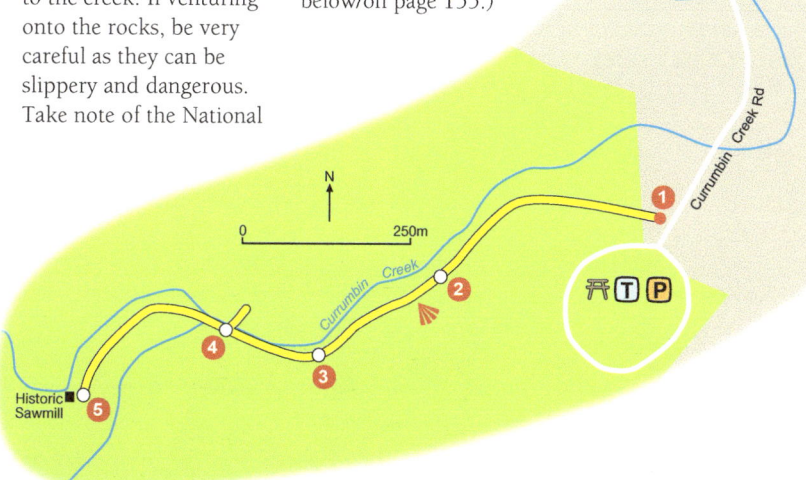

33 Mount Cougal Cascades

4 At the *Cougal Cascades* sign, take a short detour down to the creek. Return to the main path, following it for another 400 metres.

5 You'll reach an historic sawmill that worked the area from 1945 to 1954. Here you can see some of the big logs that were once taken from the area. The area became national park after the Dolan family decided to sell the land in 1983 for this purpose, rather than for development. Retrace your steps to the car park where you'll see more big logs.

Mt Cougal Cascades

33 Mount Cougal Cascades

Sawmill artifacts

Mt Cougal history – Timber industry

The only European visitors to this area in the 1860s were timber getters who found large and valuable trees, some with trunks two metres wide. Later in 1904 it was opened for settlement but was not cleared until the 1920s. By then it was considered good banana growing land and Eric Greaves planted 50 acres (20 hectares) of bananas but they did not do well due to shading by tall trees. In 1942 the sawmill was set up to cut quandong and flooded gum for banana packing boxes by local farmer John Tracey. Then in 1948 the mill was purchased by a Brisbane timber company and operated until 1954 when six months of wet weather forced its closure. The area continued to be logged until 1961. What you see today is the land that has reverted to rainforest since the banana farming in the 1930s.

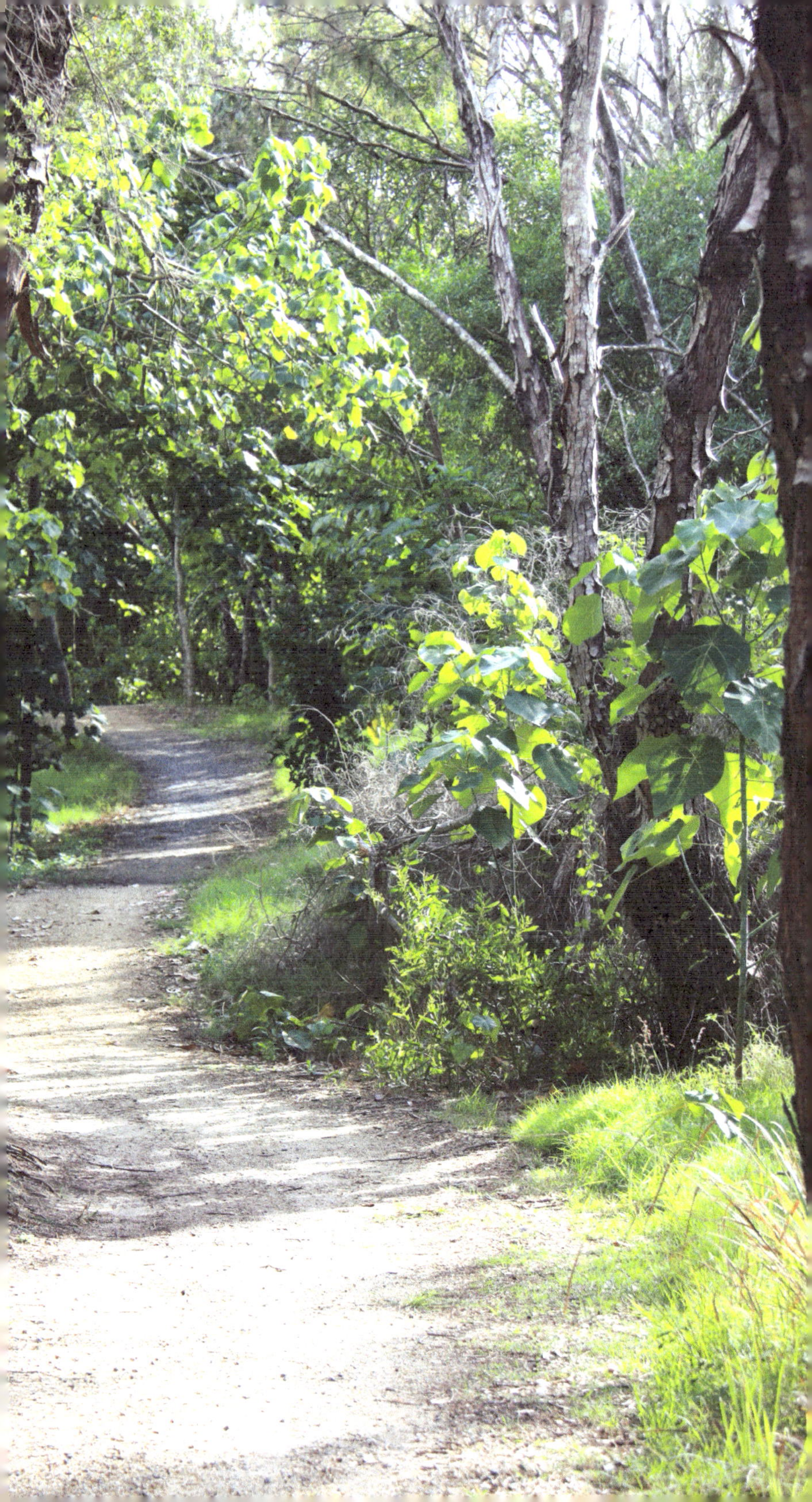

Gold Coast Wildlife

You're likely to spot plenty of wildlife when walking in Brisbane. You or your children might like to record the locations and dates of your sightings.

Masked Lapwing	Koala	Brushtail Possum
Flying-fox	Goanna	Australian White Ibis
Cicada	Eastern Water Dragon	Kookaburra
Short-necked Turtle	Rainbow Lorikeet	Pelican

Index

A-B
Apple Tree Park, 144-146
Ballaringa Lookout, 137
beaches, protecting Gold Coast, 79
beachfront markets, 25
Beree Badalla Reserve, 89-90
Beryl Carnell, 86
Bilinga, 82
Billy Rack Lookout, 69
bites, 6
Blackfellow Falls, 138
border between QLD-NSW, 72-74, 77
Botanic Gardens, 46-49
Broadbeach markets, 25
Broadbeach, 28
Brushtail possum, 157
Burleigh Heads markets, 25
Burleigh Heads, 14-21
Burleigh, 14-23
Burrawang Lookout, 108
Burrawang palm, 109
Bush turkey, 16, 19
buttress roots, 123

C
Cameron Falls, 110-113
Canyon Lookout, 135, 137, 138
Captain Cook Monument, 69, 73
Carlin Park, 73
Cascade Gardens, 42-44
Cave Creek, 150
Cedar Creek Falls, 102-104
Cedar Creek, 126-128
Centaur Remembrance Walk, 69
children, walking with, 3, 112
Cicada, 157
closures (track), 4
Coolangatta markets, 25
Coolangatta School, 81
Coolangatta, 68-70, 76-77

Coombabah Boardwalk, 62-63
Coombabah Lakelands, 58-65
Currumbin, 82-83, 84-87
Curtis Brothers, 105
Curtis Falls, 126-128
cyclists, 5
dogs, walking with, 4

D-E
Duranbah Beach, 73-74
Eastern Water Dragon, 157
Echo Beach, 16
Ed Hardy, 23
Elephant Rock, 85
environment, care for, 5, 141

F
Farmer Family Park, 86
Federation Walk, 36-39
Fig Tree Lawn, 47
first aid, 6
Flat Rock Creek, 83
Flying foxes, 43, 45, 157
food and water, 6
Francis Edward Roberts, 70

G
Geoffrey Cornish, 28
geology of Springbrook, 133
glow worms, 151
Goanna, 157
Gold Coast Botanic Gardens, 46-49
Gold Coast Hinterland Walk, 147
Gold Coast Oceanway, 6
Gold Coast Seaway, 39
Goodwin Park, 77
Goomoolahara Falls, 133
Gooroolba Falls, 135
Gowonda the Hunter, 16
grades, 3
Graeme Brien, 28
Great Walks, 147

Greenmount Hill, 69
Greenmount Walk, 70

H-I
Harley Park, 55
high-rise buildings, 31
Hinterland Great Walk, 144-146
Hoop pines, 150
Humpback whale, 21
Ibis, 157

J
Jack Evans Boat Harbour, 74
Jenyns Circuit, 106-108
Jessie MacDonald, 114
Joalah section, 127
Joe Doniger (and Park), 82

K
Kirra, 80-82
Knoll section, Tamborine NP, 110-113
Koala Track, 58-60
koalas, 61, 157
Kokoda (campaign), 44
Kokoda Track Memorial Walk, 43
Kombumerri, 16
Kookaburra, 157
Kropp family (and Park), 83
Kurrawa Beach, 27
Kurrawa Park markets, 25

L
Labrador, 54-56
Lawyer vine, 129
leeches, 6
Len Wort Park, 85
lichens, 139
lifesavers and lifeguards, 90
Little Nerang Creek, 145
Lorraine Palmer, 28

M
MacDonald Rainforest

Index

Circuit, 114-116
MacIntosh Island Park, 33
Main Beach, 34
mangroves, 47-48, 64
markets, 25
Masked lapwing, 157
Mermaid Beach, 27
Meter Maids, 35
Miami Beach, 24
Mick Schamburg, 23
Mount Cougal Cascades, 153-154
Mt Cougal timber industry, 155
Mt Tamborine, 114-115
Myrtaceae family, 49
Myrtaceae Garden, 47

N

Narrow Neck, 33
Natural Bridge, 148-150
navigation, 6
Nerang Heads, 53
Nerang River, 42-44
Ngarri-dhum Falls, 135
Nobbys Beach, 26-27
Nobbys Hill, 26
Norm Rix Park, 56
northern Gold Coast, 13-65

O-P

O'Callaghans, 105
Oceanway, 6
Pacific black duck, 44
Palm Beach Parklands, 93
Palm Beach, 88-90, 92-93
Palm Grove, 107
Pandanus palm, 17
Paula Stafford (and park), 28
Pelican, 157
photography in this book, 160
Piccabeen palms, 116, 129
Playroom, the, 99
Point Danger, 68-74
Poondahra Falls, 135
Poonyahra Falls, 135
Public transport, 3
Purling Brook Falls, 141-143, 146

Q-R

Q1, 31
QLD-NSW border, 72-74, 77
Rainbow Beach, 69
Rainbow Falls, 133
Rainbow lorikeet, 157
Razorback, 76-77
Robur track, 60
Ronnie Long, 94
Rotary Park, 43

S

safety while walking, 5
Sand Bypass Jetty, 38, 39
Sandy Creek, 110-113
Seaway, 39
Sensory Garden, 47, 48
Settlement Day Use Area, 144-146
Shark Sighting Tower, 69
sharks, 6
Short-necked turtle, 157
snakes, 6
snales, 6
Snapper Rocks, 69
southern Gold Coast, 67-99
Southport, 50-52
Spit, the, 36-39
Springbrook café, 135
Springbrook geology, 133
Springbrook National Park, 131-155
Springbrook Warrie Circuit, 132-135
Strangler fig tree, 117
sugar industry, 57
Surf Life Saving movement, 90
Surfers Paradise, 31, 32-33
Surfside Buslines, 2
Swell Sculpture Festival, 87
swimming, 6

T

Tallanbana picnic ground, 133, 135
Tallaringa Lookout (and waterfall), 137
Tallebudgera Creek, 15, 16, 96-98
Tallebudgera, 14-17, 94, 96-98
Tamarramai Falls, 137
Tamborine Mountain history, 105
Tamborine Mountain, 101-129
ticks, 6
timber industry, 155
Tom Beatson Lookout, 77
track closures, 4
Translink, 3
transport, public, 3
Tugun Desalination Plant, 95
Tumgun Lookout, 21
Tweed River, 73-74
Twin Falls, 136-138

V-W

Volunteer Marine Rescue Centres, 75
Wait-a-while, 129
Walking stick palm, 129
Wangerriburras people, 105
war, Gold Coast and, 71
Warrie Circuit, 132-135
Warringa Pool, 142, 145
water, carrying, 6
weather, 5
Whale watching, 21
Winders Park, 86
Witches Chase, 122-124
Witches Falls Distillery, 124
Witches Falls National Park, 118-125
Witches Falls Winery, 124

Y-Z

Yugambeh people, 53
Zamia Grove, 109

159

Photography in this book

All of the photographs in this book were taken by the author and the bird and animal photos on page 157, which were taken by Woodslane author, Dianne McLay are copyright of the author/provider. Photographs may not be reproduced without permission.

All of the maps were created by Pablo Candia and Kristian Palich. They are copyright Woodslane Press and may not be reproduced without permission.

About the author and Acknowledgements

About the author

Alan Ernst developed a passion for bushwalking in his youth and has continued exploring and walking bush, beach and city tracks wherever he travels. He has lived most of his life in Queensland and has been visiting the Gold Coast periodically and for holidays for over 60 years.

Acknowledgements

Thanks to all at Woodslane, particularly Andrew Swaffer, Veechi Stuart, Kate Rowe, the designers Coral Lee and Ryan Morrison and cartographers Pablo Candia and Kristian Palich and special thanks to Dianne McLay for her editorial skill and guidance.

Many thanks also for the support, encouragement, suggestions and companionship of my family and many walking friends without whose efforts the book would never have been completed.

Map symbols

MAP SYMBOLS & LEGEND

Symbol	Description	Symbol	Description
i	Tourist Information	■	Point of Interest
T	Toilet	✚	Hospital
P	Car Park		Place of Worship
☕	Cafe		Castle
🚌	Bus Stop	△ ⊙	Summit, Roundabout
	Aboriginal Site		Marina / Wharf / Jetty
	Public Art		Lake / Reservoir
	Aquarium		Creek / River
	Zoo		Footbridge
	Market		Steps / Path
1	Place of Interest		Bridge
H	Hotel		Walking Track
	Snorkeling / Diving		Walking Track / Variation
	Surfing	- - - - - - -	Ferry Service
	Skateboarding		Rocky Shoreline
	Shared Path		Railway Line, Station
	Swimming Pool / Rock Baths		Railway Station (Underground)
	Swimming Enclosure	1	Freeway / Motorway
	Beach	10	Highway
	Whale Watching		Major Road
	Ferry Terminal		Minor Road
	Sailing Club		Minor Road (Unsealed)
	Rowing Club	- - - - - -	4WD Road / Dirt Track
	Canoe Rentals		Parkland / Reserve
	Bicycle Path		Residential / Other
	Golf Course		Beach / Sand Dunes
	Picnic Area		Ocean
	BBQ		Aquatic Reserve
	Childrens Playground	N	
	Lighthouse		
●	Start / Finish of Walk		
	View Point / Lookout	0 200 m	Scale

162

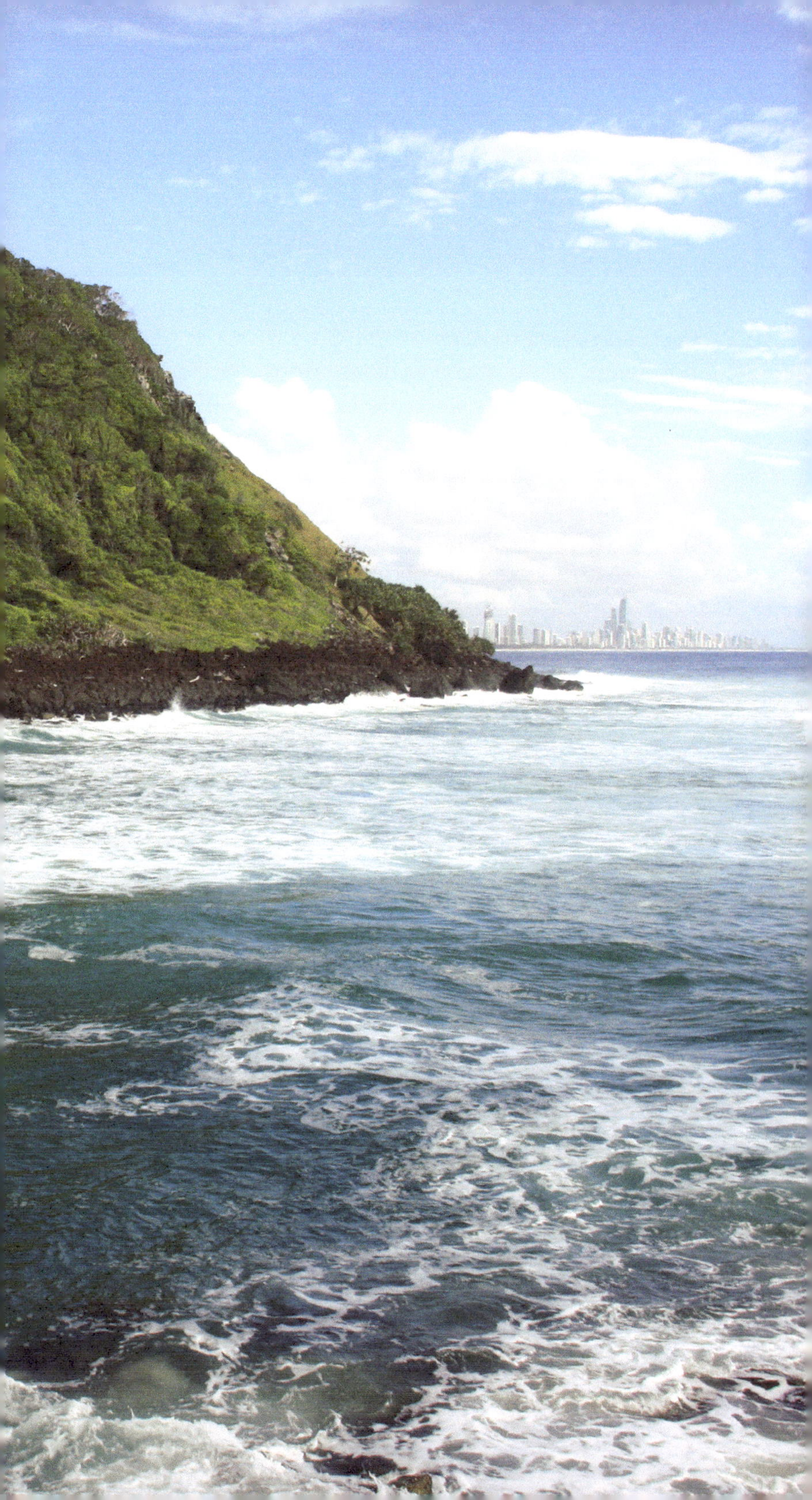

Woodslane Press & Boiling Billy

Best Bush and Beach Walks of the Gold Coast is just one of a growing series of outdoor guides from Sydney publishers Woodslane Press and sister imprint Boiling Billy. To browse through other titles available from Woodslane Press and Boiling Bill, visit www.walks.com.au and www.boilingbilly.com.au. If your local bookshop does not have stock of a Woodslane Press or Boiling Billy book, they can easily order it for you. In case of difficulty please contact our customer service team on (02) 8445 2300 or info@woodslane.com.au.

Titles include:

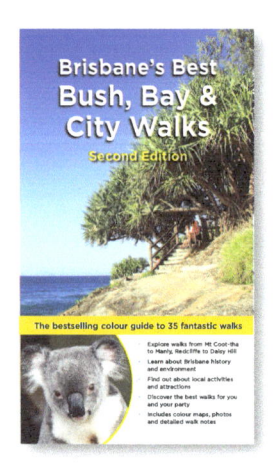

Brisbane's Best Bush, Bay & City Walks

$29.95
ISBN: 9781921874871

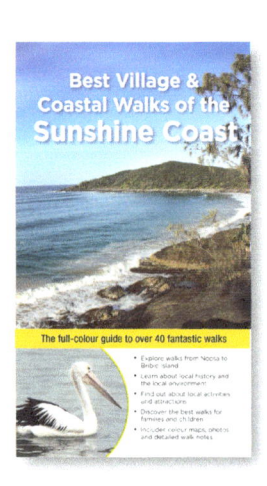

Best Village & Coastal Walks of the Sunshine Coast

$29.95
ISBN: 9781921683237

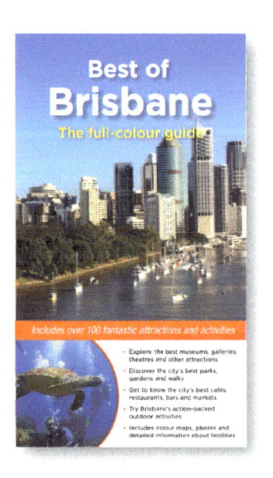

Best of Brisbane

$24.95
ISBN: 9781921606526

All Woodslane Press and Boiling Billy books are available for bulk and custom purposes. Volume copies of this and our other titles are available at wholesale prices, and custom-jacketed and even mini-extracts are possible. Contact our Publishing Manager for further information, on (02) 8445 2300 or info@woodslane.com.au.

Camping Queensland

$34.95
ISBN: 9781921606151

Camping New South Wales

$29.95
ISBN: 9781921203688

4WD Treks Close to Brisbane

$39.95
ISBN: 9781922131348

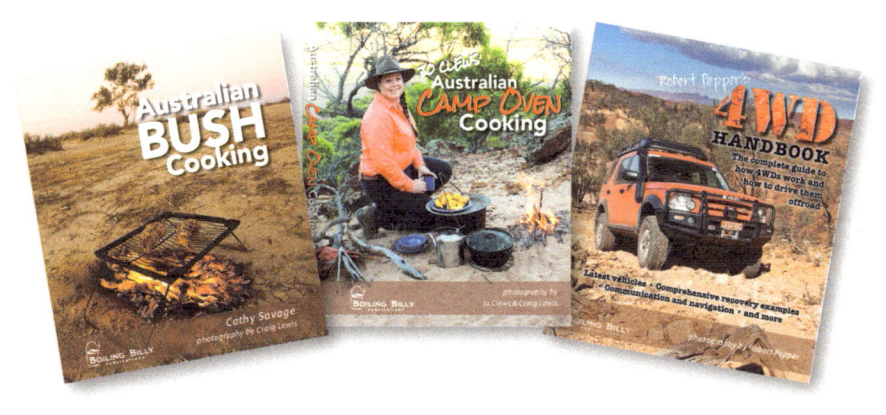

Australian Bush Cooking

$34.95
ISBN: 9781921203930

The Camp Oven Cookbook

$34.95
ISBN: 9781921874901

The 4WD Handbook

$39.95
ISBN: 9781921606175

Notes

Notes

Notes